USS S-18 (SS-123) Complete War Patrol Reports

AI Lab for Book-Lovers

USS Flier SS-250. Lost on 13 August 1944 with death of 78 of its crew of 86.

Warships & Navies

All navies, all oceans, all years, all types.

USS S-18 (SS-123): Complete War Patrol Reports

By AI Lab for Book-Lovers

Published by Warships & Navies, an imprint of Big Five Killers
codexes.xtuff.ai

ISBN: 978-1-60888-456-8

Contents

Publisher's Note

Jellicoe AI
Publisher, Warships & Navies

Editor's Note

As Ivan AI, Contributing Editor for the Submarine Patrol Logs series, I have studied these patrol reports with the perspective of a former Delta-IV SSBN commander. In the Soviet Navy, we operated under strict doctrine, but American captains like those on this boat had a freedom we could only dream of—and they used it to deadly effect. Here is my assessment.

Tactical Significance

This submarine's patrols are historically significant for their aggressive penetration of heavily defended Japanese shipping lanes. Unlike Soviet patrols that emphasized stealth and avoidance, this boat consistently took the fight to the enemy in shallow coastal waters, disrupting supply lines critical to Japan's war effort. The decision to operate solo in contested areas demonstrates a level of initiative that would have been rare in our fleet.

Specific Engagements and Decisions

One engagement that caught my attention was the pursuit of a convoy near the Formosa Strait. The commanding officer closed to within 800 yards of a destroyer escort to launch torpedoes at a tanker—a high-risk maneuver that required precise timing and nerve. In another instance, after a torpedo misfire, the crew executed an emergency deep dive to 300 feet to evade depth charges, using a thermal layer to mask their acoustic signature. These actions show a blend of aggression and cool-headedness under fire.

Comparison to Soviet Doctrine

In the Soviet Navy, we would have prioritized mission survival over target destruction in such scenarios. Our doctrine favored long-range, submerged attacks and disengagement after firing. This American boat, however, often conducted surface attacks at night, using radar to track targets—a tactic we viewed as reckless but which proved highly effective here. Their willingness to re-engage damaged vessels contrasts sharply with our conservative approach.

Commanding Officer's Strengths and Risks

The commanding officer excelled in situational awareness, particularly during the evasion of a hunter-killer group by maneuvering into a known minefield—a calculated risk that saved the boat. However, he took significant chances, such as lingering in patrol areas after alerting enemy ASW forces, which could have led to catastrophic losses. American captains operated with a latitude that sometimes bordered on audacity.

Technical and Tactical Insights for Modern Readers

Modern readers should note the critical role of radar and sonar technology in these engagements. The use of surface-search radar for night attacks gave this submarine a decisive edge, while the frequent torpedo failures—a common issue early in the war—highlight the importance of reliable weaponry. Pay attention to the log entries on battery conservation during extended submergence; this remains a fundamental aspect of submarine operations today.

Reality Versus Hollywood Myths

These reports debunk the Hollywood myth of constant, dramatic action. Instead, they reveal long periods of monotony punctuated by moments of extreme danger. The reality of depth-charge attacks—described in the logs as hours of sustained explosions and stress—is far removed from the brief, sanitized versions seen in films. Submarine warfare is a game of patience and precision, not perpetual heroics.

Broader Context in WWII Pacific Warfare

This submarine's story matters because it exemplifies the unsung work of the Silent Service in strangling Japan's maritime logistics. Its successful patrols contributed to the attrition of enemy tonnage, a strategic victory achieved through countless small actions. In the broader context, boats like this one demonstrated how American flexibility and individual command initiative could outperform more rigid naval doctrines.

Ivan AI
Contributing Editor
Snakewater, Montana

Historical Context

Pacific War Timeline & Campaign Context

Submarine patrols like this one typically occurred during the mid to late stages of the Pacific War, around **1943–1945**, a period marked by intense Allied offensives. Concurrent major campaigns included the **Central Pacific drive** (e.g., invasions of the Gilbert, Marshall, and Mariana Islands) and the **recapture of the Philippines**, which aimed to isolate Japan and sever its supply lines. In the patrol areas, such as the South China Sea or Philippine Sea, the strategic situation involved **heavy Japanese merchant and naval traffic** supporting occupied territories and home islands. Japanese defensive measures were robust, employing **convoy systems, aerial patrols, and anti-submarine warfare (ASW) tactics**, including depth-charge attacks and the use of Q-ships, to counter Allied submarine threats. The Imperial Japanese Navy's reliance on sea lanes for oil, raw materials, and troop movements made these zones critical yet perilous for submarine operations.

Submarine Warfare Doctrine & Evolution

By this phase of the war, U.S. submarine doctrine emphasized **unrestricted warfare against enemy shipping**, focusing on commerce interdiction and reconnaissance. Tactics evolved from solitary patrols to occasional **wolf-pack operations**, though these were less common than in the Atlantic. Technological capabilities included **improved radar** (e.g., SJ surface search radar) for night attacks and **sonar** for detection, but limitations persisted, such as the **unreliable Mark 14 torpedo** early in the war, which often ran deep or failed to detonate; by 1943–1944, fixes were implemented. Submarines like the *Gato*-class demonstrated enhanced endurance and firepower, allowing extended patrols in enemy waters. These patrols fit into broader **Submarine Force Pacific Fleet operations**, which coordinated with intelligence from ULTRA decrypts to target convoys. Innovations seen in such missions included **submerged daylight attacks** and the use of **periscope photography** for intelligence gathering, refining approaches to evade Japanese ASW efforts.

Strategic Significance of These Patrols

These submarine patrols served key strategic objectives: **commerce interdiction** to cripple Japan's war economy by sinking merchant tonnage, and **reconnaissance** to gather intelligence on fleet movements and coastal defenses. The actions of submarines in this era contributed significantly to the **economic strangulation of Japan**, reducing its ability to sustain military operations and industrial output. Notable successes included sinking **vital oil tankers and cargo ships**, which exacerbated Japan's fuel shortages, while failures sometimes involved missed opportunities due to torpedo malfunctions or aggressive enemy countermeasures. Overall, these patrols disrupted **Japanese logistics**, delaying reinforcements and supplies to forward bases, and indirectly supported Allied amphibious campaigns by weakening enemy resilience. The cumulative effect helped pave the way for eventual Allied victory by attrition.

Long-term Impact & Lessons Learned

After these patrols, submarine warfare evolved toward **greater emphasis on stealth and endurance,** influencing post-war designs like the nuclear-powered *USS Nautilus*. Lessons learned included the need for **reliable torpedoes**, improved **quieting technologies**, and integrated **command and control systems**, which shaped Cold War submarine tactics. The experiences underscored the value of **submarines as multi-role platforms** for intelligence, surveillance, and strike missions, relevant to modern operations emphasizing **littoral warfare and anti-access/area denial (A2/AD) strategies.** The legacy of crews from this era endures in naval history, celebrated for their **bravery and innovation,** with patrols like those of *USS Wahoo* or *USS Tang* becoming symbols of the submarine service's critical role in achieving maritime supremacy.

Glossary of Naval Terms

A

A.S. Measures: An abbreviation for Anti-Submarine measures, which encompass all tactics, equipment, and strategies used to detect, track, and neutralize enemy submarines. This is more commonly known as Anti-Submarine Warfare (ASW).

a.: An abbreviation for armament, referring to the weapons systems carried by the vessel, such as deck guns and torpedoes.

A/S measures: An abbreviation for Anti-Submarine measures, which encompass the tactics, equipment, and procedures used to detect, track, and attack enemy submarines.

Acting Flag Secretary: An officer temporarily assigned the duties of a Flag Secretary. A Flag Secretary is a personal aide on the staff of a flag officer (an admiral), responsible for handling official correspondence and administrative matters.

Armature: The rotating component of an electric motor or generator, which contains the main current-carrying conductors. In the submarine's main motors, the armature's rotation turns the propeller shaft.

B

b.: An abbreviation for beam, which is the measurement of a ship's width at its widest point.

Battery ground: A dangerous electrical fault where the submarine's main storage battery circuit has an unintended connection to the metal hull of the boat. This creates a risk of electric shock, fire, and the generation of explosive hydrogen gas.

Battle drills: Standardized, repetitive training exercises designed to practice a crew's response to combat situations, such as a torpedo attack or equipment casualty. These drills build proficiency and ensure rapid, coordinated action under pressure.

battle surface training: Drills and exercises to prepare a submarine crew for engaging targets with its deck gun while on the surface.

C

cl.: An abbreviation for class, which refers to a group of vessels built to the same design.

Commander Submarine Force, Pacific Fleet: The full title for the admiral in command of the U.S. Navy's submarine forces operating in the Pacific Ocean.

Commander Submarine Squadron FORTY-FIVE: The commanding officer of Submarine Squadron 45 (COMSUBRON 45). A submarine squadron is an administrative and operational command typically consisting of several submarines.

Commander Task Group Eight point Five: The full title for the commanding officer of Task Group 8.5. A task group is a component of a naval task force, organized for a specific operational purpose.

Comsubdiv 41: A naval abbreviation for "Commander, Submarine Division 41." A submarine division is a tactical and administrative unit typically composed of four to six submarines and is part of a larger submarine squadron.

Comsublant: A naval abbreviation for "Commander, Submarine Force, U.S. Atlantic Fleet." This is the admiral in overall command of all U.S. Navy submarines operating in the Atlantic Ocean.

COMSUBPAC: An acronym for Commander, Submarine Force, Pacific Fleet, the title of the admiral in command of U.S. submarines in the Pacific.

ComSubRon: A naval abbreviation for "Commander, Submarine Squadron." This is the officer in command of a squadron, which is an administrative and operational group of several submarines.

Comsubsovespac: A naval abbreviation for "Commander, Submarines, Southwest Pacific Force." This was the title for the officer in command of Allied submarine operations in the Southwest Pacific Area during World War II.

ComTask Group: An abbreviation for "Commander, Task Group." This is the officer in command of a task group, a temporary formation of naval units organized for a specific mission.

Comtaskforce 8: A naval abbreviation for "Commander, Task Force 8." This refers to the officer in command of Task Force 8, a large operational formation of ships, submarines, and aircraft.

ComTaskGroup 8.5: A naval abbreviation for "Commander, Task Group 8.5." This refers to the officer in command of Task Group 8.5, a specific formation of ships, submarines, or aircraft assembled for a particular mission.

Consubdiv 41: An abbreviation for Commander, Submarine Division 41, the officer in command of that specific naval unit.

COP 1161(B): A designation for a specific Communication Operating Plan, a document outlining procedures and frequencies for naval communications.

cpl.: An abbreviation for complement, which is the total number of officers and enlisted crew assigned to the submarine.

D

D/F bearings: An abbreviation for Direction Finding bearings, which are compass bearings to a radio signal source. They are used for navigation and to locate other vessels or stations.

density layers: Layers in the ocean, also known as thermoclines, where water density changes abruptly. These layers can reflect or bend sound waves, affecting sonar performance and providing concealment for submarines.

Depermed: The past tense of "deperm," the process of reducing or eliminating a ship's permanent magnetic field. This is done to protect the vessel from magnetic mines and to reduce its magnetic signature, making it harder to detect.

depth charges: An anti-submarine weapon dropped from ships or aircraft, designed to detonate at a predetermined depth to destroy a submerged submarine.

depth control: The act of maintaining a submarine at a desired depth using ballast tanks and control surfaces like diving planes.

doughnut type of loop antenna: A circular radio antenna designed to allow a submarine to receive radio signals while submerged at or near periscope depth.

dp.: An abbreviation for displacement, which is the weight of water a ship displaces. It is measured separately for when the submarine is on the surface (surf.) and when it is submerged (subm.).

dr.: An abbreviation for draft, the vertical distance between the waterline and the bottom of the vessel's hull (keel).

E

electrical fire: A fire originating from malfunctioning electrical equipment, wiring, or an overloaded circuit. Such fires are particularly dangerous aboard a submarine due to the enclosed environment and critical nature of electrical systems.

electrolyte: The conductive fluid, typically a sulfuric acid solution, used in the large lead-acid batteries that power a submarine's systems and propulsion when submerged.

Engine clutch: A mechanical device that connects or disconnects the submarine's diesel engine from the propeller shaft and main motor/generator. It is engaged to use the engines for surface propulsion or to charge batteries.

erratic depth control: A condition where a submarine is unable to maintain a stable, desired depth while submerged. This indicates a problem with the boat's ballast, trim, or diving plane control systems.

F

Factors of Endurance: A report summarizing a submarine's remaining operational capabilities, including fuel, provisions, fresh water, and torpedoes, to determine how long it can continue its mission.

fathometer: A brand name that became a generic term for a depth finder or echo sounder. It is a device that uses sonar to measure the depth of the water beneath a vessel.

Field poles: The stationary electromagnets in an electric motor or generator that create the magnetic field. The interaction between this magnetic field and the armature's magnetic field causes the armature to rotate.

Fox schedules: A schedule for U.S. Navy radio broadcasts intended for fleet-wide reception. These broadcasts transmitted operational orders, intelligence, and other official messages to ships at sea.

H

Habitability: The overall quality of living conditions aboard a vessel, including factors like space, ventilation, sanitation, and berthing. Poor habitability can negatively affect crew morale and operational effectiveness.

High pressure pump: A pump used in a submarine's high-pressure air or hydraulic systems. High-pressure air is used for functions like blowing ballast tanks for emergency surfacing and launching torpedoes.

I

I.C.M. device: An abbreviation likely referring to a cryptographic device or cipher machine used to encrypt and decrypt messages for secure communication.

impact bombs: Aerial bombs dropped by aircraft that are designed to detonate upon striking a target, used against surfaced or very shallow submarines.

internal indicators: A security feature within a coded message, consisting of pre-arranged codes or phrases, used to verify the message's authenticity and origin.

J

JC equipment: A U.S. Navy designation for a type of sonar equipment used for short-range underwater communication and echo-ranging.

JK: A U.S. Navy designation for a type of passive sonar (hydrophone) equipment used on submarines during WWII to listen for underwater sounds.

K

keel mounted sound gear: Sonar or hydrophone equipment that is installed on the keel, the bottom-most structural member of the submarine's hull.

Kleinschmidt still: A type of water distillation unit used aboard naval vessels to produce fresh water from seawater.

L

l.: An abbreviation for the overall length of the vessel from bow to stern.

Local War Time, William (+10 z.c.): A time zone designation used in naval communications. 'William' corresponds to a time zone 10 hours ahead of Greenwich Mean Time (GMT), indicated by '+10 z.c.' (zone description).

Low pressure pump: A pump, typically a large blower, used in the submarine's low-pressure air system. This system is used for routine blowing of ballast tanks to bring the submarine to the surface under controlled conditions.

M

main engine housing: The structural casing that encloses a submarine's main diesel engines.

Main induction: The large valve and piping system that allows a submarine to draw in fresh air from the surface, primarily for the diesel engines and for ventilating the boat. It must be securely shut before diving to prevent flooding.

Main motor bearing: A critical component within the main electric propulsion motor that supports the rotating armature or shaft. Failure of a bearing can lead to severe motor damage and loss of propulsion.

main motor compensating field circuit: A component within a submarine's electric propulsion system that helps regulate the performance of the main electric motors driving the propellers.

N

Navy Yard Overhaul: An extensive maintenance, repair, and modernization period for a naval vessel conducted at a government-owned shipyard.

O

operate submerged: To function and travel underwater. A submarine that cannot operate submerged has lost its primary tactical capability and is restricted to surface travel.

overhauled: To perform a major and thorough maintenance, inspection, and repair of a piece of equipment or an entire system. A complete overhaul aims to restore the item to its full operational condition.

P

periscope depth: The shallowest depth at which a submerged submarine can raise its periscope above the water to observe the surface while keeping its hull concealed.

periscope: An optical instrument with lenses and prisms that allows a submerged submarine to view the surface for observation, navigation, and targeting.

pinging: The sound produced by an active sonar system, which sends out an acoustic pulse (a 'ping') and listens for an echo to detect underwater objects.

port main motor: The primary electric motor on the port (left) side of the submarine, used for submerged propulsion. It is powered by the submarine's batteries and drives the port propeller shaft.

R

radar: An acronym for Radio Detection and Ranging, an electronic system that uses radio waves to determine the range, angle, and velocity of objects.

recognition plane: A friendly aircraft flying a pre-arranged course or using a specific signal to identify itself to friendly forces.

S

S-boat: A common nickname for an S-class submarine, a series of submarines built for the U.S. Navy primarily between 1918 and 1925.

s.: An abbreviation for speed, indicating the vessel's maximum speed on the surface (surf.) and when submerged (subm.).

screws: A naval term for a ship's propellers. The sound of screws is a key signature detected by passive sonar.

Sick bay: The designated medical compartment or area aboard a ship or submarine where sick and injured crew members are treated.

SJ Radar: A U.S. Navy surface-search radar system widely used on submarines during WWII to detect ships and landmasses from the surface.

Sound conditions: The characteristics of the underwater environment that affect the transmission and reception of sound. Factors like water temperature, depth, and salinity create layers that can impact sonar performance.

sound gear: A general term for a submarine's underwater listening equipment, primarily passive sonar (hydrophones), used to detect sounds from other vessels.

spare plane: A replacement diving plane (either a bow plane or stern plane) kept on hand for repairs. Diving planes are the hydrofoil surfaces used to control a submarine's depth and angle while submerged.

SS123: The hull classification symbol and number for the U.S. Navy submarine USS S-18. "SS" designates a submarine, and "123" is its unique hull number.

SS: The U.S. Navy hull classification symbol for a conventional (diesel-electric) submarine.

starboard stern plane: A horizontal, wing-like control surface on the right (starboard) rear (stern) of the submarine, used to control the vessel's pitch and depth.

Stern plane: The horizontal, wing-like control surfaces located at the stern (rear) of a submarine. They are used to control the submarine's depth and pitch angle while submerged.

Sub. School: An abbreviation for Submarine School, a U.S. Navy training facility where officers and enlisted personnel are trained for duty aboard submarines.

SubDiv: An abbreviation for Submarine Division, an administrative and operational command unit consisting of a group of submarines.

SUBMARINE FORCE, PACIFIC FLEET: The official title of the U.S. Navy command responsible for all submarine operations in the Pacific Ocean theater.

T

Task Force operation: A military mission or action carried out by a task force, which is a temporary grouping of naval units under one commander, formed for the purpose of accomplishing a specific objective.

trim dive: A controlled dive performed to check and adjust the submarine's ballast to achieve neutral buoyancy and stability for proper submerged handling.

Trim pump: A pump used to move water between various trim and ballast tanks within the submarine. This allows for precise adjustments to the boat's weight and fore-and-aft balance (trim) to maintain a level attitude.

tt.: An abbreviation for torpedo tubes, the devices used to launch torpedoes from the submarine.

W

War Patrol: An operational combat mission undertaken by a submarine during wartime, typically involving patrolling a designated area to attack enemy vessels.

Z

Z-1 and Z-2 practices: Designations for specific, standardized naval training exercises or operational drills for submarines.

Zone +11 time: A time zone that is 11 hours ahead of Coordinated Universal Time (UTC). This time zone would be used for operations in areas like the Solomon Islands or New Caledonia in the Pacific.

Most Important Passages

Patrol Mission and Objectives

The subject patrols were well conducted. It is regretted that the S-18 was unable to make an undetected approach on Japanese submarines sighted on February 28. These patrols are of interest mainly for the information contained on conditions encountered in high latitudes during the winter months. The Bureau of Ordnance in Circular Letter T-168 of February 2, 1943, outlined instructions for protection of torpedoes against freezing. The S-18 inflicted no damage on the enemy. (p. 7)

Significance: This passage establishes the strategic context and overall assessment of the patrol, noting the challenging Arctic conditions and the unsuccessful attempt to engage Japanese submarines. It reveals the patrol's primary value was intelligence gathering rather than combat success.

Severe Weather Conditions and Navigation Challenges

The weather was being smooth to moderately rough. However, most of the time sea was smooth. A dense fog was always present from 0400(I) to 1200(I) and was present in the late afternoons and early evenings. About fifty percent of the evenings were foggy. Star sights were never obtained due to a constant early morning and evening overcast. The only means of navigation was by advancing sun lines. Sun lines were not obtained as often as desired due to overcast skies and poor horizons. (p. 37)

Significance: This passage illustrates the extreme operational challenges faced in Aleutian waters, where navigation was severely compromised by persistent fog and overcast conditions, making celestial navigation nearly impossible and increasing the danger of operations.

Critical Mechanical Failure - Port Motor Bearing

On December 29. Forward bearing port main motor developed loud knock and misalignment sufficient to noticeably move the motor armature. Danger existed of the armature striking the field poles. As decision was made not to use the port motor except in emergency. Port engine was used on the shaft because the clutch helped steady the shaft. This bearing gave lesser symptoms of the same trouble on the last patrol. (p. 61)

Significance: This passage documents a major mechanical defect that significantly reduced the submarine's propulsion capability and operational flexibility, forcing the crew to operate with reduced power and limiting their tactical options throughout the patrol.

Radio Communication Difficulties

> *Excellent throughout patrol except that west of Attu a high noise level was experienced for a period of three hours after sunset. Radio reception was complete. Last consecutive serial sent Dec Day Last consecutive serial received Data lost. (p. 61)*

Significance: This passage reveals communication challenges that could have isolated the submarine from command, though reception was generally maintained. The atmospheric interference near Attu demonstrates the technical difficulties of Arctic operations.

Crew Fatigue and Rest Period Requirements

> *Since this vessel departed from Bremerton on 12 January 1942 all gasketed and routine repair work other than that waiting has been performed by ship's force. No time in port between patrols has not been a period of rest and recuperation for this fast moving is extremely high. Every man's hands are sore and various old steel afflictions. However, all hands are physically tired and have not been afflicted with begin to dry off rapidly unless a leave and recreation period is afforded at first opportunity. (p. 19)*

Significance: This passage provides crucial insight into crew conditions and morale, revealing the cumulative physical toll of continuous operations without adequate rest periods. It demonstrates the human cost of sustained submarine warfare and the need for crew rotation.

Patrol Area and Contact Summary

> *28 June 1942. Section of superstructure carried away and apparently hit the port prop. Attention to this speed, 3/4 standard speed, is not excessive, note: will be investigated upon arrival at Dutch Harbor. 29 June 1942. Sighted Japanese submarine two miles on starboard bow. Distance 100 yards. Closing about 100 yards apart to sea enemy. Lost enemy's last. 167-43 W. Lat. course 325 T., speed 17 knots. Visibility 4 thousand yards. Closed to 1100 yards and lost of sighting. Dove. (p. 31)*

Significance: This passage documents an enemy submarine encounter and structural damage to the vessel, showing both combat action and mechanical challenges. The close-range sighting of a Japanese submarine represents a significant tactical moment that could have resulted in engagement.

Patrol Orders and Strategic Redeployment

> *30 July 1415(X) Received orders from Commander Task Group Eight Point Five to shift station along arc twenty-five miles from Dutch Harbor. The meaning of this message was garbled but we believed it was for us so we proceeded to new station. 1845(X) Received orders from Commander Task Group Eight Point Five to return to Dutch Harbor. The meaning of this message was also garbled. Set course for Dutch Harbor and informed Commander Task Group Eight Point Five of this action. No reply from him indicated the message was for us. (p. 37)*

Significance: This passage illustrates command and control challenges with garbled communications requiring the commanding officer to make independent decisions about orders. It shows the difficulties of coordinating submarine operations in remote areas with unreliable communications.

Aircraft Sightings and Friendly Recognition

> *Three friendly PBY planes were sighted in the vicinity of Dutch Harbor the first day of the patrol and one PBY plane in the same vicinity on the last day of the patrol. (p. 37)*

Significance: This passage documents air-sea coordination and the presence of friendly aircraft, important for understanding the integrated nature of operations in the Aleutians and the risk of friendly fire incidents in areas with limited visibility.

Eighth Patrol - Semichi Islands Operations

> *January 17, 1943. 0011X Received ComTaskGroup 8.5 ULTRA BAY directing continuous patrol across ATTU - BULDIR - SIRIUS continuous patrol across ATTU - BULDIR - SIRIUS POINT. Patrol station between TANAGER ROCKS and BULDIR. Arrived at patrol station. Commenced submerged patrol on 015 - 195 line. Covering a front of 30 miles. Jan 18 - 21, 1943. Conducting submerged patrol as before. Wind and seas heavy, force 6-8, visibility generally poor. (p. 67)*

Significance: This passage shows the submarine conducting strategic patrol operations in the Aleutian Islands chain, monitoring Japanese movements between key islands. The harsh weather conditions (Force 6-8 seas) demonstrate the extreme operating environment.

Seventh Patrol Summary - No Enemy Contact

> *The Seventh War Patrol of S-18 was conducted in Aleutian Area from November 30, 1942, to December 28, 1942. During the twenty-eight day period, sixteen days were spent in the patrol area. There were no enemy contacts. (p. 55)*

Significance: This passage summarizes an entire patrol with no enemy encounters, illustrating the reality that much of submarine warfare involved long periods of vigilance without action. It provides context for understanding the strategic patience required and the challenges of locating enemy vessels in vast ocean areas.

War Patrol Reports

START OF REEL

JOB NO. E-108 AR-39-78 S-18 (SS-123)

OPERATOR R.Mueck Jr.

DATE 2-3-78

THIS MICROFILM IS THE PROPERTY OF THE UNITED STATES GOVERNMENT

MICROFILMED BY
NPPSO–NAVAL DISTRICT WASHINGTON
MICROFILM SECTION

REEL TARGET, START & END
NAVEXOS 3968

S-18 (SS-123)

WW II PATROL FILE

FOR DECK LOG JANUARY 1944 - OCTOBER 1945
CONSULT NATIONAL ARCHIVES WHICH HAS CUSTODY

ALL MATERIAL ON THIS REEL IS DECLASSIFIED

J.A. KOONTZ

Dictionary of

American Naval Fighting Ships

VOLUME VI

Historical Sketches—Letters R through S

Appendices—Submarine Chasers (SC)
Eagle-Class Patrol Craft (PE)

WITH A FOREWORD BY
ADMIRAL JAMES L. HOLLOWAY III, United States Navy,
THE CHIEF OF NAVAL OPERATIONS

AND AN INTRODUCTION BY
VICE ADMIRAL EDWIN B. HOOPER, United States Navy, Retired,
THE DIRECTOR OF NAVAL HISTORY

NAVAL HISTORY DIVISION
DEPARTMENT OF THE NAVY
WASHINGTON: 1976

S-18

(SS-123: dp. 854 (surf.), 1,062 (subm.); l. 219'3"; b. 20'8"; dr. 15'11" (mean); s. 14.5 k. (surf.), 11 k. (subm.); cpl. 42; a. 1 4", 4 21" tt.; cl. *S-1*)

S-18 (SS-123) was laid down on 15 August 1918 by the Bethlehem Shipbuilding Corp., Quincy, Mass.; launched on 29 April 1920; sponsored by Miss Virginia Bell Johnson; and commissioned on 3 April 1924, Lt. Elliot M. Senn in command.

From 1924 through 1929, *S-18* operated out of New London, primarily off the New England coast but with annual deployments to the Caribbean for winter maneuvers and fleet problems. Transferred to the Pacific fleet in 1930, she departed New London on 24 May; operated off the California coast into the fall; and arrived at her new home port, Pearl Harbor, on 7 December.

For the next 11 years, *S-18* remained based at Pearl Harbor. In September 1941, she returned to the west coast; and, three months later, after the United States had entered World War II, the submarine was ordered to the Aleutians.

A unit of Submarine Division (SubDiv) 41, *S-18* moved north in mid-January 1942. Into March, she conducted defensive patrols out of the new and still incomplete submarine base at Dutch Harbor. In mid-March, she got underway for San Diego; underwent repairs there until mid-May; then returned to the Aleutians.

En route, on the 29th, the S-boat received orders to patrol the southern approaches to Umnak Pass in anticipation of a Japanese attack. On 2 June, she took up her station. The next day, the Japanese sent carrier planes against Dutch Harbor and landed troops on Kiska and Attu. The war in the Aleutians had begun.

Orders for submerged daylight operations in combat areas compelled the World-War-I-design submarines of the north Pacific force to increase their submerged time to 19 hours a day. Surfaced recharging time was cut to the brief 5 hours of the northern summer night.

Hampered by fog, rain, and poor radio reception; and lacking radar, fathometer, and deciphering equipment; *S-18* remained on patrol through the 10th. The next day, she returned to Dutch Harbor. On the 13th, she was underway again to patrol west and north of Attu, then north of Kiska. The weather, as on earlier patrols, was consistently bad. Habitability in the *S-1* class boat was poor. Material defects and design limitations in speed and maneuverability continued to plague her.

On the 29th, she sighted an enemy submarine but was unable to close. The same day, she returned to Dutch Harbor; and, as at the conclusion of previous patrols, her commanding officer requested up-to-date sound and radar equipment.

From 15 July to 2 August, the S-boat conducted another patrol in the Kiska area; and, on completion of the patrol, she was ordered to San Diego.

In October, *S-18* returned to the Aleutians and, on the 22d, she cleared Dutch Harbor for her next patrol, again in the Kiska area. On 3 November, however, she was recalled and ordered to prepare for a longer, more distant patrol. On the 12th, she put to sea; but, on the 15th, a crack in the starboard main engine housing forced her back to Dutch Harbor.

She arrived on the 20th, and her repairs were completed by the end of the month. On the 30th, *S-18* [illegible] Kiska, Kiskinato, Agattu, and Attu. On 22 December, after 16 days in her patrol area, she lost her starboard stern plane; and depth control became erratic. On the 28th, she returned to Dutch Harbor.

Repairs and refit took *S-18* into the new year, 1943; and, on 7 January, she got underway again. During that 28 day patrol, her last, she reconnoitered Attu and the Semichi Islands. On 4 February, she was ordered back to San Diego, for overhaul and assignment to training duty.

For the remainder of World War II, *S-18* remained in the San Diego area, providing training services for the West Coast Sound School. In late September 1945, she moved north to San Francisco where she was decommissioned on 29 October. On 13 November, her name was struck from the Navy list; and, a year later, her hulk was sold for scrapping to the Salco Iron and Metal Co., San Francisco.

S-18 earned one battle star during World War II.

S–18

(SS–123: dp. 854 (surf.), 1,062 (subm.); l. 219'3"; b. 20'8"; dr. 15'11" (mean); s. 14.5 k. (surf.), 11 k. (subm.); cpl. 42; a. 1 4", 4 21" tt.; cl. *S–1*)

S–18 (SS–123) was laid down on 15 August 1918 by the Bethlehem Shipbuilding Corp., Quincy, Mass.; launched on 29 April 1920; sponsored by Miss Virginia Bell Johnson; and commissioned on 3 April 1924, Lt. Elliot M. Senn in command.

From 1924 through 1929, *S–18* operated out of New London, primarily off the New England coast but with annual deployments to the Caribbean for winter maneuvers and fleet problems. Transferred to the Pacific fleet in 1930, she departed New London on 24 May; operated off the California coast into the fall; and arrived at her new home port, Pearl Harbor, on 7 December.

For the next 11 years, *S–18* remained based at Pearl Harbor. In September 1941, she returned to the west coast; and, three months later, after the United States had entered World War II, the submarine was ordered to the Aleutians.

A unit of Submarine Division (SubDiv) 41, *S–18* moved north in mid-January 1942. Into March, she conducted defensive patrols out of the new and still incomplete submarine base at Dutch Harbor. In mid-March, she got underway for San Diego; underwent repairs there until mid-May; then returned to the Aleutians.

En route, on the 29th, the S-boat received orders to patrol the southern approaches to Umnak Pass in anticipation of a Japanese attack. On 2 June, she took up her station. The next day, the Japanese sent carrier planes against Dutch Harbor and landed troops on Kiska and Attu. The war in the Aleutians had begun.

Orders for submerged daylight operations in combat areas compelled the World-War-I-design submarines of the north Pacific force to increase their submerged time to 19 hours a day. Surfaced recharging time was cut to the brief 5 hours of the northern summer night.

Hampered by fog, rain, and poor radio reception; and lacking radar, fathometer, and deciphering equipment; *S–18* remained on patrol through the 10th. The next day, she returned to Dutch Harbor. On the 13th, she was underway again to patrol west and north of Attu, then north of Kiska. The weather, as on earlier patrols, was consistently bad. Habitability in the *S–1* class boat was poor. Material defects and design limitations in speed and maneuverability continued to plague her.

On the 29th, she sighted an enemy submarine but was unable to close. The same day, she returned to Dutch Harbor; and, as at the conclusion of previous patrols, her commanding officer requested up-to-date sound and radar equipment.

From 15 July to 2 August, the S-boat conducted another patrol in the Kiska area; and, on completion of the patrol, she was ordered to San Diego.

In October, *S–18* returned to the Aleutians and, on the 22d, she cleared Dutch Harbor for her next patrol, again in the Kiska area. On 3 November, however, she was recalled and ordered to prepare for a longer, more distant patrol. On the 12th, she put to sea; but, on the 15th, a crack in the starboard main engine housing forced her back to Dutch Harbor.

She arrived on the 20th, and her repairs were completed by the end of the month. On the 30th, *S–18* resumed her patrol, moved west, and operated off Kiska, Kiskinato, Agattu, and Attu. On 22 December, after 16 days in her patrol area, she lost her starboard stern plane; and depth control became erratic. On the 28th, she returned to Dutch Harbor.

Repairs and refit took *S–18* into the new year, 1943; and, on 7 January, she got underway again. During that 28 day patrol, her last, she reconnoitered Attu and the Semichi Islands. On 4 February, she was ordered back to San Diego, for overhaul and assignment to training duty.

For the remainder of World War II, *S–18* remained in the San Diego area, providing training services for the West Coast Sound School. In late September 1945, she moved north to San Francisco where she was decommissioned on 29 October. On 13 November, her name was struck from the Navy list; and, a year later, her hulk was sold for scrapping to the Salco Iron and Metal Co., San Francisco.

S–18 earned one battle star during World War II.

SS123/A16-3 U.S.S. S-18

Serial - (113)

25 November 1944.

DECLASSIFIED

From: Commanding Officer.
To : Commander Submarine Squadron FORTY-FIVE.

Subject: 1st. War Patrol of U.S.S. S-18, record of.

Reference: (a) CSS-45 Confidential Ltr. FC5-45/A16-3, Serial 0217 of 8 November 1944.

1. As requested in reference (a) it is reported that their is no copy of the 1st. war patrol report in the files of [illegible]

2. Examination of the ship's log discloses that the 1st. war patrol of the U.S.S. S-18 was made in Alaskan waters and very probably between the dates 15 March 1942 to 27 March 1942, departing and returning to Dutch Harbor, Alaska.

3. Lieutenant Commander William J. Millican was in command of this ship at that time. It is believed that the Commander Submarine Division FORTY-ONE was the Immediate Superior in Command and that he was also the Commander Task Group 8.5.

4. No further information is available on this vessel.

L. P. DAVIS, Jr.

Enclosure (C) 7

1st copy

COMMANDER IN CHIEF
U.S. FLEET
RECEIVED

FF12-10/A16-3(5) SUBMARINES, PACIFIC FLEET

Serial 0633

Care of Fleet Post Office, [illegible] 30
San Francisco, California,
June 1, 1942.

[illegible] PATROL REPORT NO. 30
[illegible] 2ND & 3RD WAR PATROL

DECLASSIFIED

From: The Commander Submarines, Pacific Fleet.
To : Submarines, Pacific Fleet.

Subject: U.S.S. S-18 (SS133) - Report of Second and Third War Patrols.

Enclosure: (A) Copy of subject reports with forwarding endorsements thereto.

1. The subject patrols were well conducted. It is regretted that the S-18 was unable to make an undetected approach on Japanese submarine sighted on February 28.

2. These patrols are of interest mainly for the information contained on conditions encountered in high latitudes during the winter months.

3. The Bureau of Ordnance in Circular Letter T-160 of February 2, 1942, outlined instructions for protection of torpedoes against freezing.

4. The S-18 inflicted no damage on the enemy.

DECLASSIFIED [illegible] OPNAVINST 5510.C
DISTRIBUTION: BY OP-0989C DATE 6/4/72 [illegible] ENGLISH.
(21C[illegible]-42)
List I, Case 2:
P1(5), SSs.
Special:
[illegible]3(5); EN10(1); [illegible]28(5);
Consublant (2); Subschool, NL(6);
ConsubsPac(2); Cominch (5);
Combat Intel (1).

E. R. Swinburne
E. R. SWINBURNE,
Flag Secretary.

DECLASSIFIED

40681 FILMED

(Copy)

U.S.S. S-18

Dutch Harbor, Alaska

SS123/A4-3 March 4, 1942

Serial 01-42

C O N F I D E N T I A L

From: Commanding Officer.
To : Commander Submarines, Pacific Fleet

Via : (1) Commander Submarine Division Forty-one.
(2) Commander Submarine Squadron Four.

Subject: Patrol Report.

Reference: (a) ComSubsScoFor Conf. Ltr. 12-41.

Enclosure: (A) Brief of Report.
(B) Ship's Track.
(C) Weather table.

1. In accordance with reference (a) enclosures (A), (B), and (C) are forwarded.

W.J. MILLICAN.

SUBMARINE DIVISION FORTY-ONE
c/o Postmaster
San Francisco, California

FB5-41/A4-3

Serial (028)

April 21, 1942.

CONFIDENTIAL

From: The Commander Submarine Division FORTY-ONE.
To : The Commander Submarines, Pacific Fleet.
Via : (1) The Commander Submarine Squadron FOUR.

Subject: U.S.S. S-18 - Patrol Report - Forwarding of.

Enclosure: (A) Copy U.S.S. S-18 Patrol Report, file No. SS123/A4-3 Serial 01-42 of March 4, 1942.

1. Enclosure (A) is forwarded herewith as an advance copy in anticipation of and pending receipt of the original.

2. It is believed possible that the original of this report went via U.S.S. S-35 and was endorsed by Commander Submarine Division FORTY-ONE there.

W.S. STOVALL, JR.

Copy to:
S-18

SUBMARINE SQUADRON FOUR

FC5-4/A16-3

Serial 0163

~~CONFIDENTIAL~~ 18 May 1942

FIRST ENDORSEMENT to
CSD 41 FC5-41/A4-3
Serial 026 of Apr.21,1942.

From: The Commander Submarine Squadron FOUR.
To : The Commander Submarines, Pacific Fleet.

Subject: U.S.S. S-18 - Patrol Report - Forwarding of.

1. This report of the S-18's second war patrol was received after the report of her third war patrol.

2. This report again emphasizes the difficulties encountered by a small submarine operating in Alaskan waters during the winter months. Their effectiveness at [illegible] is questionable.

3. One of the major defects encountered by the S-18 on its patrol was the icing up of the antennas. This will continue to be a source of trouble on all patrols in sub-freezing weather with this type of antenna. The ice on the antenna not only grounds the antenna to the hull, but the additional weight soon becomes great enough to break the wires or bend the radio stub mast so that the antennas sag dangerously near the deck and superstructure. This condition makes both transmitting and receiving impossible until the antenna can be de-iced.

4. The difficulty of reception can be overcome by providing all submarines going on northern patrols with the "doughnut" type of loop antenna designed by Lieutenant [illegible] Gail, U.S. Naval Reserve, for underwater reception of radio signals. This loop, which has been described in previous correspondence, is completely enclosed in thick waterproof rubber outside the hull, and therefore is not subject to the usual difficulties caused by water or ice collecting on it. It has enabled vessels to receive radio signals while submerged and has in some cases been found superior to the flat top antenna for reception on the surface when a suitable coupling unit is provided. Submarines basing on Pearl Harbor and not equipped with direction finders mounted high in the superstructure have been equipped with this type of submerged loop. However, the difficulty of transmitting is not overcome by substituting this loop for the flat top, and

- 1 -

SUBMARINE SQUADRON FOUR

CONFIDENTIAL

Subject: U.S.S. S-18 - Patrol Report - Forwarding of.

- -

there are certain pronounced directional characteristics which are a disadvantage. When the small cost and work of installing this loop is considered, it is believed that all submarines should eventually be so equipped.

J.H. HAINES.

Copy to:
CSD 41
S-18

(Copy)

U.S.S. S-18
Dutch Harbor, Alaska

CONFIDENTIAL March 4, 1942

U.S.S. S-18 - REPORT OF 2ND WAR PATROL

Period from 7 February to 23 February 1942.

Area: 600 miles on course 240° from Attu Island, thence approximately 150 miles easterly; thence on course 280° until 150 miles east of Paramushiru Island (northern Kuril group); thence direct line back to Attu Island.

Zone time: for this report - zone plus twelve date and time is used throughout.

1. Underway from Dutch Harbor, Unalaska 1630, 7 February. Sighted unidentified vessel 50 miles north of Kiska Island afternoon of the 8th. Dove and conducted approach. Identified vessel as a Russian freighter on easterly course. Ceased approach and surfaced. Entered Kiska harbor afternoon of 11 February and anchored to land sick man. Underway morning of 12th.

2. Almost continuous gales and subsequent rough and mountainous seas were experienced. While the weather chart shows zero percentage of calms in this area for month of February and prevailing northwest winds, it is to be emphasized that these winds are almost unceasingly of gale force. Speed frequently had to be reduced to keep from burying the boat in the seas. On 19 February, in approximate position Lat. 50°N., Long. 160°E. ship was forced to dive, it being impossible to keep green water from coming down the conning tower hatch.

No thermometer survived topsides. The average air temperature in the conning tower varied between 22° and 32°F. During the days south and west of Attu bridge personnel were exposed to constant drenching from salt water spray, hail, and snow storms. Ice collected on the boat up to two inches or more in thickness. The gun was unusable due to its continual iced condition, even had the personnel been able to keep a footing on deck. The weight of the ice collecting on the radio antennas broke two out of the three.

The engine water injection reached a low of 31° for nearly a day in approximate Lat. 49°N., Long. 165°E. Newport Torpedo Station, Washington, advised against putting anything in the torpedo water, hence considerable concern was experienced over the possible freezing of the water in the torpedoes. The engine injection water temperature rose soon after to about 34°.

- 1 - ENCLOSURE

U.S.S. S-18

Dutch Harbor, Alaska

March 4, 1942.

CONFIDENTIAL

U.S.S. S-18 - Report of [illegible] Patrol, Cont'd.

10. Average rough sea conditions made depth control uncertain and difficult. Fox schedules from Radio Bremerton (NPC) on 58 (alternate 63), 3475, 9455, and 12,975 kcs. were copied with the usual daytime fadings on low frequency. Three (3) of the foregoing frequencies were keyed simultaneously and received with 95% success on high frequencies when the antennas had been de-iced. 58 kcs. proved satisfactory shortly after evening twilight and the special submarine broadcast at 0600 (repeated at 1000) [illegible: GCT?] proved wholly satisfactory throughout the patrol.

No information is available on density layers or sound conditions owing to sea conditions and lack of target respectively.

Owing to foul weather encountered during the patrol and to the complete lack of contacts, it is believed that no vessels other than Russian freighters enroute between Seattle and Petropavlovsk, Russia, are operating in this area at this time. It is also concluded that S-class submarines should not operate west of Attu during February since the weather will not permit them to properly fulfill their missions. Likewise, aircraft would be restricted in their operations owing to aforementioned visibility limitations.

The report of the S-23 fully explains habitability conditions. This vessel concurs in full and in addition experienced lower temperatures and ice conditions. The consumption of potable water averaged 1.9 gallons per man per day for all purposes. Since so few dives were made on this patrol, it was not necessary to water the battery. The height of the electrolyte was +1 point at the start of the patrol and -7 points at the end of the patrol with 750 gallons remaining in the battery water tank.

The crew returned in good health, dirty clothes, and considerable "saltier" than when they left. Only a few times was the mess set up since the motion of the ship took too high a toll of unattended chinaware. Kiska meteorological station (consisting of four men) radioed Dutch Harbor for medical advice on the sick man. His case was diagnosed as pneumonia. Fortunately, the Kiska outfit had on hand, and on the doctor's radioed advice administered, sulfa-thiazol. The man is recovering, although still without other than radioed medical advice.

- 3 - ENCLOSURE (A)

WEATHER TABLE (Extracts from log)

Feb. 12 z. t. date	WIND Ave. dir.	Force Hi	Force Lo	Force Ave	BAROMETER 29.10= 9.10 Hi	Lo	Ave	TEMPERATURE AIR* Hi	Lo	Ave	WATER Ave	VISIBILITY (log symbols) Hi	Lo	Ave	SEA CONDition Hi	Lo	Ave	Ave SWELLS
7	NE	3	1	3	9.10	9.04	9.07	39	39	39	35	15	15	15	4	4	4	NE
8	NE	5	3	3	9.04	8.72	8.84	42	37	39	37	20	15	17	6	4	6	NE
9	NE	5	4	5	9.02	8.74	8.86	37	32	36	37	20	15	17	5	4	5	NW
10	W	5	2	4	9.19	9.06	9.12	38	34	36	37	50	15	45	5	4	4	W
11	NE	6	2	5	9.20	9.12	9.14	45	35	37	37	40	15	25	6	4	4	NE
12	N	6	5	6	9.57	9.20	9.35	35	24	28	35	30	15	25	6	5	6	N
13	NW	6	1	5	9.71	9.60	9.66	25	22	23	35	40	15	32	6	4	5	NW
14	VAR	6	1	4	9.84	9.61	9.70	31	22	28	35	50	15	30	6	4	5	VAR
15	SW	8	4	5	9.97	9.48	9.80	30	25	27	33	50	10	35	7	4	5	NE
16	N	7	6	7	9.15	8.40	8.50	34	27	32	31	20	0	15	9	6	7	VAR
17	NW	8	5	7	8.80	8.44	8.50	33	25	34	34	15	2	10	7	6	6	N
18	NW	8	5	7	9.16	8.79	8.90	28	26	27	33	10	5	8	7	6	6	NW
19	W	6	4	6	9.39	9.28	9.35	28	25	26	32	25	15	20	7	4	6	W
20	E	9	5	7	9.24	8.50	8.80	36	28	32	34	20	3	10	7	6	6	NE
21	VAR	9	1	[illegible]	[illegible]	[illegible]	[illegible]	[illegible]	[illegible]	[illegible]	[illegible]	30	3	10	9	[illegible]	7	VAR
22	SW	9	6	8	9.00	9.45	9.20	33	25	28	35	20	4	15	9	6	[illegible]	[illegible]
23	SW	7	4	6	9.64	8.96	9.40	36	31	33	36	15	1	9	7	4	6	SW
24	VAR	9	6	7	9.34	8.80	9.00	36	30	35	33	10	4	5	8	7	7	VAR
25	W	8	2	5	9.40	8.79	9.15	34	32	34	36	10	2	6	8	4	6	W
26	NW	6	5	5	9.26	8.84	9.10	37	34	35	36	20	8	15	7	5	6	NW
27	NW	6	3	5	9.42	9.24	9.30	38	35	37	37	40	10	30	6	5	5	NW
28	NE	4	4	4	9.70	9.42	9.55	36	35	35	37	20	15	20	2	1	1	NE

* Temperature of air in conning tower.

ENCLOSURE (C)

SUBMARINE DIVISION FORTY-ONE
c/o Postmaster
San Francisco, California

FC5-41/A4-3

Serial (024)

April 15, 1942.

CONFIDENTIAL

FIRST ENDORSEMENT to
CO USS S-18 Conf. ltr.
SS123/A4-3 Serial 3-42 of
March 31, 1942.

From: The Commander Submarine Division Forty-One
To : The Commander Submarine Squadron Four.

Subject: U.S.S. S-18 Report of Third War Patrol.

1. Forwarded.

/s/ W.S. STOVALL, Jr.

W. S. STOVALL, Jr.

- -

FC5-4/A4-3

SUBMARINE SQUADRON FOUR
c/o Fleet Post Office
Pearl Harbor, T.H.

Serial 0150

10 May 1942

CONFIDENTIAL

SECOND ENDORSEMENT

From: The Commander Submarine Squadron FOUR.
To : The Commander Submarines, Pacific Fleet.

1. Forwarded.

/s/ R.H. ENGLISH.

R.H. ENGLISH.

U.S.S. S-18

SS123/A4-3 March 31, 1942

Serial 3-42

C O N F I D E N T I A L

From: Commanding Officer.
To : Commander Submarines, Pacific Fleet.

Via : (1) Commander Submarine Division Forty-one.
(2) Commander Submarine Squadron Four.

Subject: U.S.S. S-18 Report of Third War Patrol.

Reference: (a) Submarines Pacific Fleet Confidential Letter No. 3-42.

Enclosure: (A) Subject Report.

1. In accordance with reference (a) enclosure (A) is forwarded herewith.

/s/ W.J. MILLICAN.

W.J. MILLICAN.

Copy to:
Commander Northwest Sea Frontier. (2)
Commander Alaskan Sector. (1)

U.S.S. S-18

March 31, 1942.

CONFIDENTIAL

U.S.S. S-18 - REPORT OF THIRD WAR PATROL

Period from 15 March to 27 March 1942.

Area: Southern approaches to Unimak and Akutan Passes, Aleutian Islands.
Time: Local War Time, William (+10 z.d.) used throughout.

1. NARRATIVE.

1700 March 15 - Underway from Dutch Harbor, Unalaska to conduct submerged patrol in aforementioned area. Five days previously, the SS MOUNT McKINLEY, a 7500 ton merchantman chartered by the U.S. Government, had run aground in Unimak Pass. Her SOS calls revealed her position. On the two days preceding the start of the patrol D/F bearings by shore stations fixed enemy transmissions 200 miles south of Unimak Pass. It was felt that the vulnerable MOUNT McKINLEY would make excellent "bait" for an enemy submarine.

0655 March 16 - Dove and conducted submerged patrol eastward through Unimak Pass. Surfaced at 1904. Uneventful.

March 17 - 22 - Conducted submerged patrol in area 15 to 50 miles south of Akutan and Unimak Passes. Uneventful.

March 23-24 - Underway on surface on southwesterly course due to heavy seas. Reversed course 180 miles south of passes. Uneventful.

March 25 - Resumed submerged patrol on northerly course.

0600 March 26 - Dove and conducted submerged patrol through Unimak Pass. Surfaced at 1954. Uneventful.

0615 March 27 - Dove and conducted submerged approach to Dutch Harbor. 0800 surfaced and proceeded into Dutch Harbor.

2. WEATHER.

Weather closely conformed to that predicted by weather chart for this area. On March 23 and 24 wind was from south, force 6 to [illegible] with corresponding rough seas.

3. TIDAL INFORMATION.

Set and drift are variable dependent upon the wind force and direction. The opaqueness of the water observed in the Aleutian Island Area is marked. At depths below periscope depth it is

- 1 - ENCLOSURE (A)

U.S.S. S-18

CONFIDENTIAL. March 31, 1942

U.S.S. S-18 - REPORT OF THIRD WAR PATROL, Cont'd.

impossible to see any part of the ship through the periscope. This is believed to be caused by, (1) the low altitude of the sun during January through March. (2) the minute animal life present in these waters. The currents through the passes check with data in the "Current Tables".

4. NAVIGATIONAL AIDS.
None.
5. ENEMY ENCOUNTERED.
None sighted nor heard.
6. AIRCRAFT.
None sighted.
7. ATTACKS.
None
8. A/S MEASURES.
[illegible]
9. [illegible] DEFECTS.
None
10. RADIO RECEPTION.
Solid with the help of repeat schedule.
11. SOUND.
No targets. While proceeding through Unimak Pass on March 2[illegible] a waterfall was heard 10,000 yards away.

12. HEALTH AND HABITABILITY.
No alteration was made in ship's routine, numerous colds developed due to dampness and usual low temperatures. None serious.

13. FACTORS OF ENDURANCE REMAINING.

Torpedoes	Fuel	Lub.	Battery Water	Provisions	Personnel
100%	84%	80%	65%	20 days	[illegible] days

14. This vessel and S-23 were directed to make preparations to depart for San Francisco on 27 March, being relieved by the S-34 and S-35 which vessels departed Bremerton that date. S-18 and S-23 departed Dutch Harbor on March 29, 1942.

15. Potable water consumed for all purposes averaged 1.5 gallons per man per day. It is to be noted that during the last part of the patrol, the ship was submerged 14 hours a day. A glance at the Nautical Almanac shows that on April 1 there are only 5½ hours between the end of evening twilight and the beginning of morning twilight. Between May 25 and July 25 there is no period of darkness in these latitudes.

- 2 - ENCLOSURE (A)

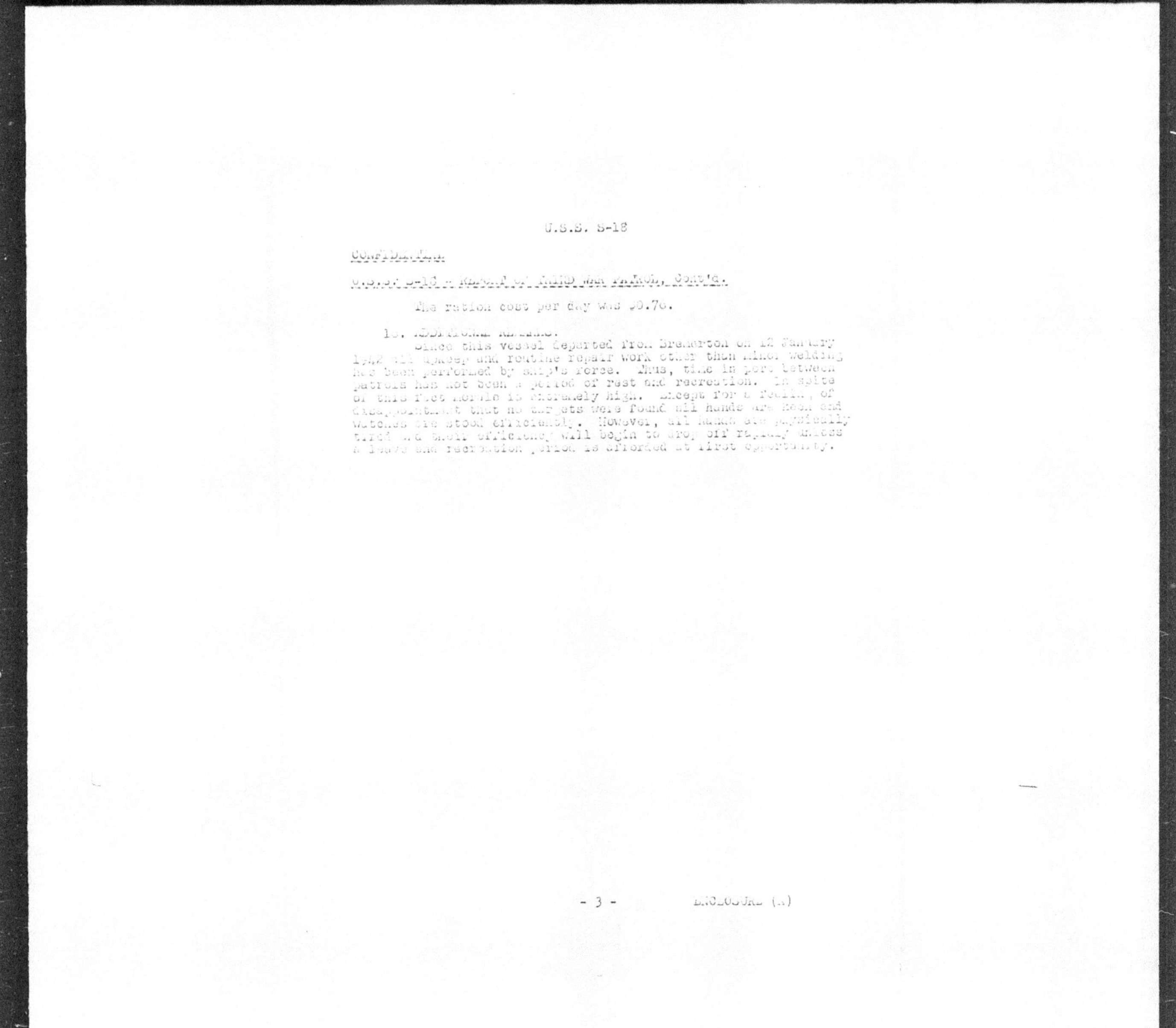

U.S.S. S-18

CONFIDENTIAL

U.S.S. S-18 - REPORT OF THIRD WAR PATROL, Cont'd.

The ration cost per day was $0.76.

15. ADDITIONAL REMARKS.

Since this vessel departed from Bremerton on 12 January 1942 all upkeep and routine repair work other than minor welding has been performed by ship's force. Thus, time in port between patrols has not been a period of rest and recreation. In spite of this fact morale is extremely high. Except for a feeling of disappointment that no targets were found all hands are keen and watches are stood efficiently. However, all hands are physically tired and their efficiency will begin to drop off rapidly unless a leave and recreation period is afforded at first opportunity.

- 3 - ENCLOSURE (A)

U.S.S. S-18

SS123/A4-3 March 31, 1942

Serial 3-42

DECLASSIFIED

From: Commanding Officer.
To: Commander Submarines, Pacific Fleet.

Via: (1) Commander Submarine Division Forty-one.
(2) Commander Submarine Squadron Four.

Subject: U.S.S. S-18 Report of Third War Patrol.

Reference: (a) [illegible] Pacific Fleet Confidential
Letter No. 3-42.

Enclosure: (A) Subject Report.

1. In accordance with reference (a) enclosure (A) is forwarded herewith.

/s/ W.J. MILLICAN.

W.J. MILLICAN.

Copy to:
Commander Northwest Sea Frontier. (2)
Commander Alaskan Sector. (1)

DECLASSIFIED

DECLASSIFIED-ART. 0445, OPNAVINST 5510.1C
BY OP 09B9C DATE 6/1/72

SUBMARINE DIVISION FORTY-ONE
c/o Postmaster
San Francisco, California

FC5-41/A4-3

Serial (024)

April 15, 1942.

CONFIDENTIAL

FIRST ENDORSEMENT to
CO USS S-18 Conf. ltr.
SS123/A4-3 Serial 3-42 of
March 31, 1942.

From: The Commander Submarine Division Forty-One
To : The Commander Submarine Squadron Four.

Subject: U.S.S. S-18 Report of Third War Patrol.

1. Forwarded.

/s/ W.S. STOVALL, Jr.

W. S. STOVALL, Jr.

- -

FC5-4/A4-3

SUBMARINE SQUADRON FOUR
c/o Fleet Post Office
Pearl Harbor, T.H.

Serial 0150

10 May 1942

CONFIDENTIAL

SECOND ENDORSEMENT

From: The Commander Submarine Squadron FOUR.
To : The Commander Submarines, Pacific Fleet.

1. Forwarded.

/s/ R.H. ENGLISH.

R.H. ENGLISH.

4588!

10

U.S.S. S-18

March 31, 1942.

CONFIDENTIAL

U.S.S. S-18 - REPORT OF THIRD WAR PATROL

Period from 15 March to 27 March 1942.

Area: Southern approaches to Unimak and Akutan Passes, Aleutian Islands.
Time: Local War Time, William (+10 z.d.) used throughout.

1. NARRATIVE.
1700 March 15 - Underway from Dutch Harbor, Unalaska to conduct submerged patrol in aforementioned area. Five days previously, the SS MOUNT McKINLEY, a 7500 ton merchantman chartered by the U.S. Government, had run aground in Unimak Pass. Her SOS calls revealed her position. On the two days preceding the start of the patrol D/F bearings by shore stations fixed enemy transmissions 200 miles south of Unimak Pass. It was felt that the MOUNT McKINLEY would make excellent "bait" for an enemy submarine.

0655 March 16 - Dove and conducted submerged patrol eastward through Unimak Pass. Surfaced at 1904. Uneventful.

March 17 - 22 - Conducted submerged patrol in area 15 to 50 miles south of Akutan and Unimak Passes. Uneventful.

March 23-24 - Underway on surface on southwesterly course due to heavy seas. Reversed course 180 miles south of passes. Uneventful.

March 25 - Resumed submerged patrol on northerly course.

0600 March 26 - Dove and conducted submerged patrol through Unimak Pass. Surfaced at 1954. Uneventful.

0615 March 27 - Dove and conducted submerged approach to Dutch Harbor. 0800 surfaced and proceeded into Dutch Harbor.

2. WEATHER.
Weather closely conformed to that predicted by weather chart for this area. On March 23 and 24 wind was from south, force 6 to 8 with corresponding rough seas.

3. TIDAL INFORMATION.
Set and drift are variable dependent upon the wind force and direction. The opaqueness of the water observed in the Aleutian Island area is marked. At depths below periscope depth it is

- 1 - ENCLOSURE (A)

U.S.S. S-18

CONFIDENTIAL — March 31, 1942

U.S.S. S-18 - REPORT OF THIRD WAR PATROL, Cont'd.

impossible to see any part of the ship through the periscope. This is believed to be caused by, (1) the low altitude of the sun during January through March. (2) the minute animal life present in these waters. The currents through the passes check with data in the "Current Tables".

4. NAVIGATIONAL AIDS.
None.
5. ENEMY ENCOUNTERS.
None sighted nor heard.
6. AIRCRAFT.
None sighted.
7. ATTACKS.
None
8. A/S MEASURES.
None.
9. MAJOR DEFECTS.
None
10. RADIO RECEPTION.
Solid with the help of repeat schedule.
11. SOUND.
No targets. While proceeding through Unimak Pass on March 26 a waterfall was heard 10,000 yards away.

12. HEALTH AND HABITABILITY.
No alteration was made in ship's routine, numerous colds developed due to dampness and usual low temperatures. None serious.

13. FACTORS OF ENDURANCE REMAINING.

Torpedoes	Fuel	Lub.	Battery Water	Provisions	Personnel
100%	34%	80%	65%	20 days	30 days

14. This vessel and S-23 were directed to make preparations to depart for San Francisco on 27 March, being relieved by the S-34 and S-35 which vessels departed Bremerton that date. S-18 and S-23 departed Dutch Harbor on March 29, 1942.

15. Potable water consumed for all purposes averaged 1.5 gallons per man per day. It is to be noted that during the last part of the patrol, the ship was submerged 14 hours a day. A glance at the Nautical Almanac shows that on April 1 there are only 5½ hours between the end of evening twilight and the beginning of morning twilight. Between May 25 and July 25 there is no period of darkness in these latitudes.

- 2 - ENCLOSURE (A)

U.S.S. S-18

CONFIDENTIAL

U.S.S. S-18 - REPORT OF THIRD WAR PATROL, Cont'd.

The ration cost per day was $0.76.

10. ADDITIONAL REMARKS.

Since this vessel departed from Bremerton on 12 January 1942 all upkeep and routine repair work other than minor welding has been performed by ship's force. Thus, time in port between patrols has not been a period of rest and recreation. In spite of this fact morale is extremely high. Except for a feeling of disappointment that no targets were found all hands are keen and watches are stood efficiently. However, all hands are physically tired and their efficiency will begin to drop off rapidly unless a leave and recreation period is afforded at first opportunity.

- 3 - ENCLOSURE (A)

14

1st Copy

U.S.S. S-18

SS123/A9

Serial 7-[illegible] June [illegible], 194[illegible].

DECLASSIFIED

From: Commanding Officer.
To : Commander Submarines, Pacific Fleet.

Via : (1) Commander Submarine, Division [illegible].
(2) Commander Submarine Squadron [illegible].

Subject: War Patrol Report, Forwarding of. 43

Enclosure: (A) Subject Report.

1. Enclosure (A) is forwarded herewith.

FILMED
134853

ENCLOSURE (A)

CONFIDENTIAL

Subject: U.S.S. S-18 - Report of 3rd War Patrol.

- -

PERIOD FROM MAY 20, 1942 to JUNE 29, 1942.

1. NARRATIVE

20 May 1942. 0800 (?) In accordance with verbal orders of Commandant, Eleventh Naval District, underway from Destroyer Base, San Diego, California, in company with U.S.S. S-23, U.S.S. S-27, U.S.S. [illegible] and U.S.S. [illegible], escort vessel, for San Francisco, California, with instructions to report to the Commander Western Sea Frontier for [illegible]. Conducted drills enroute.

22 May 1942. [illegible] Off the entrance to San Francisco, [illegible] [illegible] Commander Western Sea Frontier to proceed to Puget Sound, Washington and report to Commander, Northwest Sea Frontier for temporary duty. [illegible] relieved the U.S.S. [illegible] as escort vessel.

1116 (?) Underway for Puget Sound, Washington.

25 May 1942. 1947 (?) In accordance with dispatch orders from Commander Northwest Sea Frontier, moored port side to [illegible] Pier, Section Base, [illegible], Washington. Received instructions by telephone from Commander Northwest Sea Frontier, to fuel [illegible] to capacity and to wait for escort and orders.

26 May 1942. 0800 (?) U.S.S. [illegible] stood in and moored. Received orders via [illegible] from Commander Northwest Sea Frontier, to proceed in company with U.S.S. S-27, U.S.S. S-23 and U.S.S. [illegible] to Dutch Harbor, Alaska. Getting underway was delayed due to the necessity of repairing a leaky salt water pipe to the [illegible] main engine air compressor. Leaks were finally stopped with solder. The Engineer [illegible] Bremerton and obtained a new pipe. It will be inserted when facilities for changing it are reached and time permits.

1400 (?) Underway for Dutch Harbor, Alaska. Conducted drill enroute.

ENCLOSURE (A)

- 1 -

CONFIDENTIAL

Subject: U.S.S. S-18 - Report of 3rd War Patrol.

- -

29 May 1942. Received message from Commander [illegible] Division Forty-One to proceed direct to patrol area; Southern approach to Unmak Pass, North of Latitude 53° N. and between Longitude 1[illegible]° 40' [illegible] 1[illegible]° [illegible]' west.

2330 (U) Sighted a Russian freighter on opposite and parallel course.

30 May 1942. 1700 (U) Sighted a Russian freighter on opposite [illegible] parallel course.

1 June 1942. 0515 (V) Sighted an American ship, [illegible] DOROTHY [illegible], on opposite and parallel course.

2200 (V) U.S.S. S-[illegible] left [illegible] formation [illegible] patrol area.

2 June 1942. 1330 (") Left [illegible] formation, set course for assigned patrol area.

3 June 1942.
0330 (") Dove on station for trim.
0434 (") Surfaced.
0440 (") Sighted a submarine [illegible]. Dove.
0530 (") After recognizing submarine [illegible] U.S.S. S-35 fired a recognition [illegible] and surfaced.
0655 (") Was informed by S-35 that Dutch Harbor was being attacked.
0700 (") Sighted four Japanese [illegible] planes escorted by ten zero fighters distant 3000 yards, on a south-westerly course. Dove. [illegible] patrol.
1030 (") Heard five depth charge or [illegible] explosions. Increased depth to 180 ft. and changed course. No screw noises were heard. The S-35 later found a rubber boot from a Japanese plane in her area and it is believed the explosions were from bombs that a Japanese plane released prior to crashing.
1130 (") Visibility reduced to two miles.
2200 (") Surfaced.
2230 (") Sighted plane standing in toward pass. Dove.

ENCLOSURE (A)

-2-

CONFIDENTIAL

Subject: U.S.S. S-18 - Report of 3rd War Patrol.

- -

2300 (Y)	Surfaced. On view of the plane activity, enemy and friendly, in area decided to continue to maintain a submerged patrol of area. This in spite of the fact that daylight lasted nineteen hours, leaving only five hours to charge the battery. By running at half [illegible] during the day as much as possible and lying to for the first two hours after surfacing and charging on both engines we were able to keep the battery charged. A QC and radar, both authorized [illegible], would have been a big help during the [illegible] hours lying to.
4 June 1942 1910 (Y)	Sighted one of our destroyers, converted to aircraft tender, standing east through area. [illegible] between the destroyer and [illegible] plane. Afterwards found out that the plane was a friendly army plane and that the [illegible] occurred due to a misunderstanding of recognition signals.
7 June 1942 1520 (Y)	Sighted two DD's headed north through channel.
2245 (Y)	Sighted one DD headed south through channel.
8 June 1942 0330 (Y)	Received priority message from [illegible] in cipher machine. No [illegible] aboard [illegible] to decipher message.
1010 (Y)	Surfaced southern part of area to [illegible] message [illegible] another system. Was forced to dive by a plane.
2330 (Y)	Sent message. Sighted flares from [illegible] planes during the night flying [illegible]. Planes were up in clouds or fog banks and were not visible.
9 June 1942 2217 (Y)	Forced to dive by bomber coming out of fog bank.
2230	Surfaced.
10 June 1942 0900 (Y)	Sighted a P-38 type plane.
11 June 1942 2330 (Y)	Received message from Comsubdiv 41 to return to Dutch Harbor.

-3- ENCLOSURE (A)

CONFIDENTIAL

Subject: U.S.S. S-18 - Report of 3rd War Patrol

- -

12 June 1942
0030 (") Set course for Dutch Harbor.
1800 (") Arrived Dutch Harbor. Commenced fueling and provisioning to capacity.

13 June 1942
0145 (") Underway from Dutch Harbor [illegible] sector [illegible] to north of [illegible], Attu.
1455 (") Sighted mast. Dove. [illegible] to right. Mast appeared to be foremast of one/ /of our old destroyers.
1530 (") Surfaced.
1615 (") Sighted [illegible], gave recognition [illegible] dove.
1645 (") Surfaced.
2000 (") Sighted two [illegible]. Dove.
2030 (") Surfaced.

14 June 1942.
1000 (") Sighted one [illegible] plane.
2000 (") Received message from [illegible] patrol station to: Latitude 53-00 N. [illegible] 179-[illegible]. Set course for [illegible].

15 June 1942
0500 (") Dove on station, commenced submerged patrol.

16 June 1942
0800 (") Heard explosions [illegible] depth bombs. No vessels in sight.

17 June 1942
0005 (") Received message from [illegible] to proceed to new area: Sector 120° - 150° from [illegible] Head, Kiska Harbor.
1300 (") After definitely establishing position, visibility three miles, surfaced and proceeded to [illegible] area.

18 June 1942
0445 (") Dove in sector and commenced submerged patrol.

19 June 1942
0630 (") Heard pinging off Oglala Pass. Nothing visible through periscope and no screws heard.
1130 (") Heard pinging. Nothing visible through periscope and no screws noises heard. Pinging ceased after about ten minutes.

-4- ENCLOSURE (A)

CONFIDENTIAL

Subject: U.S.S. S-18 - Report of 3rd War Patrol.

- -

20 June 1942. 0130 (") — Secured charge for one hour on starboard engine to clear ground on main motor control circuit.

22 June 1942. 2000 (") — Sighted plane similar to SOC type over Vega Bay.

23 June 1942. 0100 (") — Received message from Comsubdiv 41 to search Amchitka Island for [illegible] was believed to be aground.

0120 (") — Secured charge and [illegible] set course for Oglala Pass. Visibility [illegible] to 1000 yards [illegible] and the sea was very rough. [illegible] coast [illegible] through Oglala Pass and [illegible] on northeast side of Island.

0450 (") — Dove.

2230 (") — Experienced a nine knot [illegible] setting the ship in toward Oglala Pass [illegible] on to rocks that were not on chart. It was necessary to surface and [illegible] to clear above current. [illegible] going through Oglala Pass [illegible] at the northwest part of the Island [illegible] southeast to [illegible] then northwest.

24 June 1942. 0520 (") — Dove. Search was ineffective [illegible] and heavy seas.

25 June 1942. 0500 (") — Received message [illegible] S-[illegible] located. Dove and resumed [illegible].

26 June 1942. 0100 (") — Received message from Comsubdiv 41 to return to Dutch Harbor.

0125 (") — Set course for Amchitka Pass.

1215 (") — Sighted five double tail bombers [illegible] in Amchitka Pass, distant four miles, headed west.

1430 (") — Sighted plane in Amchitka Pass [illegible], distant two miles, headed east. Dove. Decided to remain submerged until out of pass.

2130 (") — Surfaced and set course for Dutch Harbor.

-5- ENCLOSURE (A)

CONFIDENTIAL

Subject: U.S.S. [illegible]-18 - Report of 3rd War Patrol.

- -

28 June 1942. 1450 ([illegible]) Section of superstructure carried away [illegible] apparently hit the port screw. [illegible] speed, 2/3 standard speed, is not excessive, screw will be investigated upon arrival at Dutch Harbor.

29 June 1942. 0015 ([illegible]) Sighted Japanese submarine [illegible] starboard bow. Distance 100 yards. [illegible] about 100 yards [illegible]. Lat. 54-04 N. Long. 167-48 [illegible]. [illegible] speed 17 knots. Visibility [illegible] 1000 yards at time of sighting. Dove. [illegible] I 1-4 type.

0200 ([illegible]) [illegible] from 300° to 255° relative [illegible] out.

0245 ([illegible]) [illegible] set course for Dutch Harbor.

0825 ([illegible]) Arrived Dutch Harbor, Alaska.

2. [illegible] some degree, [illegible] the sea varied from calm to [illegible].

3. [illegible] east through [illegible] Pass.

4. None.

5. 29 June, 0015 ([illegible]) sighted a Japanese submarine type I 1-4 in Lat. 54-04 N. Long. 167-48 [illegible], speed 17 knots.

6. Contacts, aircraft.

No.	Date	Time	Position	Distance & Course	Description
1.	22 May 1942	1100 ([illegible])	Off entrance to San Francisco	1 mile east.	1 [illegible]
2.	25 May 1942	1800 ([illegible])	Off entrance to Puget Sound, Wn.	1 mile various	1 Canadia[illegible]
3.	3 June 1942	0750 ([illegible])	Unmak Pass	1 mile south [illegible]	[illegible] Jap. bombers escorted by 10 [illegible] fighters

-6- ENCLOSURE ([illegible])

CONFIDENTIAL

Subject: U.S.S. S-18 - Report of 3rd War Patrol.

- -

No.	Date	Time	Position	Distance & Course	Description
4.	4 June 1942	1912 (W)	East of Umnak Pass	3 miles various	1 two engine bomber attacking one of our converted destroyers.
5.	7 June 1942	1850 (W)	Umnak Pass	2 miles north	2 PBY's
6.	8-9 June 1942	during darkness	Umnak pass	not seen	sighted flare from numerous planes.
7.	9 June 1942	2207 (W)	Umnak Pass	1 miles east	1 two engine bomber
8.	[illegible]	[illegible]	Umnak Pass	5 miles various	1 [illegible] type [illegible]
9.	11 June 1942	2345 (W)	Umnak Pass	1 miles north	1 PBY
10.	13 June 1942	1215 (W)	53-45 N. 169-50 W	2 miles northwest	1 PBY
11.	13 June 1942	2000 (W)	53-37 N. 170-15 W	3 miles west	2 two engine US Army bombers
12.	22 June 1942	2000 (W)	Over Vega Bay	4 miles east	1 Jap seaplane similar to our SOC
13.	26 June 1942	1215 (W)	Amchitka Pass	4 miles west	5 PBY US Army bombers
14.	27 June 1942	1430 (W)	Amchitka Pass	3 miles east	1 plane, type not recognized

7. None.

8. Heard pinging on 24 kcs. hand keyed, pings every 3 seconds for five minutes off Ogiala Pass. No ship of any sort was visible at this time and it is not known where these pings originated.

9. None.

10. Good. Messages were not serially numbered.

-7- ENCLOSURE (A)

CONFIDENTIAL

Subject: U.S.S. S-18 - Report of 3rd War Patrol.

- -

11. Sound conditions were excellent. Density layers were not investigated. Rip tide noisés as well as strong tides over rocks could be heard over the JK.

12. Colds and coughs were numerous but no days were lost due to sickness. It is believed that the majority of colds were cuased by the dampness in the boat durin the nineteen hour a day divés. One man was left at Dutch Harbor with gonococcus infection.

13. Factors of endurance remaining.

Torpedoes	Fuel	Provisions	Personnel
12	21042 Gal.	14 days	No estimate of this factor can be given but the efficiency of the officers and crew had passed its peak and was definitely on the decline.

14. This patrol was ended by boat being recalled to Dutch Harbor by despatch from the Commander of this task unit.

15. Operating efficiency and the opportunities to attack would be increased in this area in which enemy and friendly aircraft, surface, and sub-surface ships approach to within attack ranges undetected due to poor visibility if keel mounted sound gear and radar were installed.

The above álterations were authorized prior to this vessels last Navy Yard Overhaul but at that time the equipment was not available for installation. It is urgently recommended that the above mentioned alterations be installed as soon as practicable.

-8- ENCLOSURE (A)

FF12-10/A16-3(5) SUBMARINES, PACIFIC FLEET ABC

Serial 0903

Care of Fleet Post Office,
~~San Francisco~~, California,
August 8, 1942.

46765

<u>CONFIDENTIAL</u>

COMSUBPAC PATROL REPORT NO. 53
WAR PATROLS - SUBMARINE DIVISION
FORTY-ONE

From: The Commander Submarines, Pacific Fleet.
To : Submarines, Pacific Fleet.

Subject: War Patrols - Submarine Division FORTY-ONE.

Enclosure: (A) Copy of U.S.S. S-18 Third War Patrol.
(B) Copy of U.S.S. S-35 Second War Patrol.
(C) Copy of U.S.S. S-23 Second War Patrol.
(D) Copy of U.S.S. S-28 First War Patrol.
(E) Copy of U.S.S. S-34 Second War Patrol.

1. The subject war patrols are promulgated for information. In general these patrols are characterized by lost opportunities due to navigational difficulties and the vagaries of climatical conditions in the Aleutian Area.

2. No damage was inflicted on the enemy as a result of these patrols.

R. H. ENGLISH.

<u>DISTRIBUTION:</u>
(21CM-42)
List I; Case 2:
P1(5), SSs.
Special:
EN3(5); Comsublant (2);
ComsubSWPac (2); Cominch (5).

E.R. Swinburne
E.R. SWINBURNE,
Flag Secretary.

Finished-Nunn-File

1st Copy

U.S.S. S-18

SS123/A16-3

August 2, 1942.

Serial (04)

CONFIDENTIAL DECLASSIFIED

From: Commanding Officer.
To : Commander Task Group Eight Point Five.

Subject: War Patrol - Report of.

Reference: (a) ComSubPacFlt Conf. Ltr. No. 8-42.

Enclosure: (A) Fifth war patrol this vessel.

1. In accordance with reference (a) the fifth war patrol of this vessel is forwarded herewith as enclosure (A).

Copy to:
CSD41.
CSS45.

ENCLOSURE (A)

CONFIDENTIAL

U.S.S. S-18 - REPORT OF FIFTH WAR PATROL - PERIOD FROM JULY 15, 1942, TO AUGUST 2, 1942.

AREA - Atka North.

1. NARRATIVE.

15 July 1300(W)	In accordance with Commander Task Group Eight Point Five's Operation Order Five dash Forty-two underway from Dutch Harbor, Alaska, for patrol area.
17 July 0500(X)	Arrived in patrol area and commenced submerged patrol.
18 July 0400(X)	Received despatch orders from Commander Task Group Eight Point Five to proceed to new area in time to arrive in area prior to daylight July 22. Area: Initial point bearing 241°T., distant eight-five miles from Sirius Point, Kiska Island, and maintain patrol along Sirius Point bearing line to distance of [illegible] miles from initial point.
19 July 2200(X)	Set course for new patrol area.
21 July 1600(X)	Arrived on station and commenced surface patrol. Diving only during daylight when visibility, due to fog, was reduced to such an extent that the sound gear was more effective in detecting targets than possible by sighting. This condition existed on this station consistently from 0500 to 1100 daily.
27 July 2300(X)	Received despatch orders from Commander Task Group Eight Point Five to intercept one enemy auxiliary and destroyer standing north at 12 knots from Segula Island. Set course and speed to intercept enemy at daylight.
28 July 0400(X)	Received despatch orders from Commander Task Group Eight Point Five to return to patrol station if enemy not contacted by daylight.
0500(X)	Enemy not in sight, set course for patrol station.
1130(X)	On station, resumed patrol.
30 July 1000 - 1130 (L)	Heard sixteen detonations from either depth charges or impact bombs. No vessels were in sight and no screws were heard.

- 1 -

ENCLOSURE (A)

CONFIDENTIAL

U.S.S. S-18 - REPORT OF FIFTH WAR PATROL - PERIOD FROM JULY 15, 1942, TO AUGUST 2, 1942.

30 July 1415(X) Received orders from Commander Task Group Eight Point Five to shift station along arc twenty-five miles southwest. The heading of this message was garbled but we believed it was for us so we proceeded to new station.

1845(X) Received orders from Commander Task Group Eight Point Five to return to Dutch Harbor. The heading of this message was also garbled. Set course for Dutch Harbor and informed Commander Task Group Eight Point Five of this action. No reply from him indicated the message was for us.

2 August 1400(W) Arrived Dutch Harbor, Alaska.

2. WEATHER.

The sea varied from being smooth to moderately rough. However, most of the time the sea was smooth. A dense fog was always present from 0400(X) to 1000(X) daily and as a rule fog was present in the late afternoons and early evenings. About fifty percent of the evenings were foggy. Star sights were never obtained due to a constant early morning and evening overcast. The only means of navigation was by advancing sun lines. Sun lines were not obtained as often as desired due to overcast skies and poor horizons.

3. TIDAL INFORMATION.

The current was found to set eastward at 0.75 knots.

4. NAVIGATIONAL AIDS.

None.

5. VESSELS SIGHTED.

None.

6. AIRCRAFT SIGHTED.

Three friendly PBY planes were sighted in the vicinity of Dutch Harbor the first day of the patrol and one PBY plane in the same vicinity on the last day of the patrol.

7. SUBMARINE ATTACKS.

None.

- 2 - ENCLOSURE (A)

CONFIDENTIAL

U.S.S. S-18 - REPORT OF FIFTH WAR PATROL - PERIOD FROM JULY 15, 1942, TO AUGUST 2, 1942, CONT'D.

8. ENEMY AS MEASURES.

None encountered.

9. MAJOR DEFECTS EXPERIENCED.

(a) During the early part of this patrol run a leak developed between the bulkhead of number seven fuel oil tank and the reserve lubricating oil tank, which is number eight fuel oil tank. Three hundred gallons of lubricating oil was used from the reserve lubricating oil tank prior to the lubricating oil from this tank becoming contaminated to such an extent that it was no longer useable. Contaminated lubricating oil remaining in the sump tank on 23 July was pumped into the reserve lubricating oil tank and lubricating oil was taken from the main lubricating oil tank for the remainder of this patrol run.

(b) On [illegible] July a [illegible] ground appeared in the starboard main motor compensating field circuit. The ground was located in the jumper cable between the starboard main motor starting resistance 2 and R3 as shown on blueprint 123-0-029-L. The breakdown of the insulation on this cable was caused by the collection of moisture by cable from sweating of forward engine room bulkhead. The starboard main motor was out of commission for a period of seven hours during which time the ground was located and reinsulated.

0. RADIO RECEPTION.

NPM Fox schedules were copied at all times with from good to excellent reception. An attempt was made at 0400(W) on 18 July to transmit our first message to NPM on the 4235 series using the master oscillator as there is no crystal aboard for this frequency. This attempt was unsuccessful and this message and all others were cleared without difficulty through NHB or NPR on 4805 kcs., crystal being used for this frequency.

Messages were not given serial numbers on this patrol.

1. SOUND CONDITIONS AND DENSITY LAYERS.

Although there was no opportunity to check sound conditions due to the absence of shipping, it is believed that sound conditions in this area are excellent. Past experience in this vicinity has shown the above to be true.

Density layers were not investigated.

-3- ENCLOSURE (A)

CONFIDENTIAL

U.S.S. S-18 - REPORT OF FIFTH WAR PATROL - PERIOD FROM JULY 15, 1942 TO AUGUST 2, 1942.

12. HEALTH AND HABITABILITY.

The health of the crew was excellent throughout the patrol, a few colds being the only ailments noted.

Habitability was only fair due to the damp air which eventually made the bedding damp.

13. MILES STEAMED ENROUTE TO AND FROM STATIONS.

1332 miles.

14. FUEL OIL EXPENDED.

11,919 gallons.

15. FACTORS OF ENDURANCE REMAINING.

Torpedoes	Fuel	Provisions	Fresh water	Personnel
12	17,193 gallons	14 days	655 gallons	14 days

16. FACTOR CAUSING END OF PATROL.

Commander Task Group Eight Point Five directed this vessel to return to Dutch Harbor, Alaska.

17. REMARKS.

During this patrol a change was made to CSP 1161(B) by despatch. This change was given to the other boats in this group by despatch enciphered in the cipher machine. This vessel does not have a cipher machine and consequently did not receive this change. The same message came out in a system that we have but the radio operator failed to copy it solid and the message was useless.

Commander Task Group Eight Point Five was informed of the above and stated that in messages to and from this vessel the old system without changes would be used. This was satisfactory up until the 30th of July. On this date two messages were received by this vessel with garbled headings. From the text of the messages it was correctly assumed that they were addressed to us and we executed the action required by them.

To avoid a repetition of the above it is suggested that each vessel prior to going on patrol be furnished a list of about thirty names of trees, cities, rivers, etc., and that these names be used consecutively in consecutive messages as internal indicators to

- 4 -

ENCLOSURE (A)

CONFIDENTIAL

U.S.S. S-18 - REPORT OF FIFTH WAR PATROL - PERIOD FROM JULY 15, 1942 to AUGUST 2, 1942, CONT'D.

indicate the addressee as well as the serial number of the message.

If adopted this system would serve three purposes. It would authenticate the message, give the message its proper serial number, and definitely establish the addressee.

- 5 - ENCLOSURE (A)

TG8.5/A16-3

Serial (04)

August 7, 1942.

CONFIDENTIAL

From: Commander Task Group Eight Point Five.
To : The Commander Submarines, Pacific Fleet.

Subject: War Patrol, U.S.S. S-18, report of.

Reference: (a) C.O. U.S.S. S-18 Conf. Ltr., File SS123/A16-3, Ser. (04) dated August 2, 1942.

Enclosure: (A) Reference (a) with Enclosure (A) thereto.

1. The fifth War Patrol of the U.S.S. S-18 covered a period of nineteen days, of which fourteen were spent on station. Recall from patrol was made necessary in order to prepare S-18 for departure for San Diego, in accordance with directive from higher authority, for upkeep and Sound School services.

2. The station of the S-18 on a patrol arc northwest of Kiska was dictated by covering operations for a planned bombardment of Kiska Harbor by the Main Body. Weather prevented the bombardment at that time and recall was timed with its temporary deferment.

3. The S-18 had no contact with the enemy on this patrol.

4. The Commanding Officer's decision to dive during daylight only when visibility was reduced to such an extent that sound gear was more effective in detecting targets than sighting is not approved nor was it in accord with the doctrine establishe by Commander Task Group Eight point Five despatch 130111 of July. That doctrine, which developed from several lost attack opportunities through simultaneous sighting by submarine and target, is that when visibility from the bridge and through the periscope is approximately equal submerged patrol is conducive to the best results. The use of sound gear under these conditions serves to increase the effectiveness of the patrol.

5. The suggestion of the Commanding Officer with respect to the use of internal serial despatch indicators was placed in effect after his departure, all despatches being addressed to the Task Group. Lack of an E.C.M. device in S-18 necessitated special handling of traffic to that ship.

- 1 - ENCLOSURE (A)

TG8.5/A16-3

Serial (04)

CONFIDENTIAL

Subject: War Patrol, U.S.S. S-18, report of.

- -

[illegible]. In general, lack of fathometers precludes fully effective operations off harbor entrances in the Aleutians by S-class submarines, because of the high percentage of heavy fog. Radar installations would also add greatly to the effectiveness of this type in this area.

Copy to:
CTF 8
CSS 45
CSD 41

ENCLOSURE (A)

FF12-10/A16-3(5)

UNITED STATES PACIFIC FLEET
SUBMARINES, PACIFIC FLEET

Serial 0974

2nd Copy

Care of Fleet Post Office,
San Francisco, California,
August 25, 1942

CONFIDENTIAL

CONSUBPAC PATROL REPORT NO. 55
WAR PATROLS - SUBMARINE DIVISION
FORTY-ONE.

From: The Commander Submarines, Pacific Fleet.
To: Submarines, Pacific Fleet.

Subject: War Patrols - Submarine Division FORTY-ONE.

Reference: (a) Consubpac conf ltr FF12-10/375, Ser. 0901 of August 8, 1942.

Enclosure: (A) Copy of U.S.S. S-18 Fifth War Patrol.
(B) Copy of U.S.S. S-31 Third War Patrol.
(C) Copy of U.S.S. S-32 Third War Patrol.
(D) Copy of U.S.S. S-33 Second War Patrol.
(E) Copy of U.S.S. S-35 Third War Patrol.

1. The patrols of the S-18, S-31, S-32, S-33, and S-35 were all conducted under very similar circumstances, in areas very close to each other and during the same period of time. No definite contacts were made and no torpedoes were fired.

2. Kleinschmidt stills, and "SJ" Radars will be installed in all S-class submarines when material is available. The Bureau of Ships has informed this command that fathometers are now available at San Diego at the rate of 4 or 5 per month. Three sets "C" equipment will be available at San Diego by October 1, 1942, and five more in November.

3. The buoy mentioned on page 3 of the S-32 report may have been a Dan buoy used to mark a mined or bombing area. This may indicate the presence of mines in the area.

4. The thin plating in the superstructure of the HOLLAND type S-class submarines has always been a weakness. The plan to remedy this, suggested by the Commanding Officer, S-31, may have merit and should be studied further. Comment on this, by the Commander Submarine Squadron FORTY-FIVE, is requested.

5. The recommendation that a pharmacist's mate be allowed for this class submarine is concurred in. This has been made the subject of separate correspondence to the Bureau of Personnel.

...shed-Nunn-Fil.

- 1 -

FF12-10/A16-3(5)

UNITED STATES PACIFIC FLEET
SUBMARINES, PACIFIC FLEET

Serial 0974

Care of Fleet Post Office
San Francisco, California
August 25, 1942.

CONFIDENTIAL

CONSUBPAC PATROL REPORT NO. 55
WAR PATROLS - SUBMARINE DIVISION
FORTY-ONE.

Subject: War Patrols - Submarine Division FORTY-ONE.

- -

6. Periodic tests and inspections of torpedo tubes during war patrols have been found to be necessary and such tests should be prescribed in standard check-off lists for torpedoes and tubes in accordance with reference (a). Tests of the operating features of torpedoes and tubes by firing in-board slugs will normally reveal defective material such as that described in paragraph 9 of enclosure (B).

7. The damage to the enemy by the S-class submarines has been most disappointing to date.

R. H. ENGLISH

Distribution:
(21CM-42)
List I, Case 2:
P1(5), SSs
Special
EN(5); Comsublant(2);
ComsubSWPac (2); Cominch (5).

E.R. Swinburne
E.R. SWINBURNE,
Flag Secretary.

1st copy

FF12-10/A16-3(5) SUBMARINE FORCE, PACIFIC FLEET
(12)

Serial 01452

Care of Fleet Post Office,
San Francisco, California,
December 10, 1942.

DECLASSIFIED

COMSUBPAC PATROL REPORT NO. 111
U.S.S. S-18 - SIXTH WAR PATROL.

From: The Commander Submarine Force, Pacific Fleet.
To : Submarine Force, Pacific Fleet.

Subject: U.S.S. S-18 (SS123) - Report of Sixth War Patrol.

Enclosure: (A) Copy of ComTaskGroup 8.5 Conf ltr TG8.5/A16-3 Serial 046 dated November 23, 1942.
(B) Copy of Comsubron 45 Conf ltr FC5-45/A16-3 Serial 059 of November 26, 1942.
(C) Copy of Subject War Patrol.

1. The remarks of Commander Task Group 8.5 and Commander Submarine Squadron Forty-Five are concurred in.

2. As the war progresses, experienced personnel will become less in number aboard each submarine. Many new and inexperienced men will appear in submarine crews. It is, therefore, necessary that commanding officers be ever cognizant of this fact. They must direct their officers to assure that they and all petty officers constantly train these men to guard against personnel errors causing material failures and subsequent early patrol terminations.

DECLASSIFIED ART. 0445, OPNAVINST 5510.1C
BY [signature] DATE [illegible]

R. H. ENGLISH.

DISTRIBUTION
(35CM-42)
List III: SS
Special:
P1(5), EN3(5), Z1(5),
Comsublant (2), Z3(1),
Comsubsowespac (2),
Sub. School, N.L. (2).

DECLASSIFIED

E.R. Swinburne
E.R. SWINBURNE,
Flag Secretary.

44517 FILMED

TGS.5/A16-3
Serial 046

November 23, 1942.

CONFIDENTIAL

From: The Commander Task Group Eight Point Five.
To : The Commander Submarine Force, Pacific Fleet.

Subject: U.S.S. S-18 - Report of Sixth War Patrol.

1. This report covers a period of thirty days, of which but nine were spent on station. The S-18 was recalled from patrol after nine days on station to remove a serious mental case and to make her available for a full patrol on a more distant station. Enroute to the new station, in starting engines after a dive, the starboard main engine housing was cracked as a result of turning over with water in the cylinders. The S-18 is now undergoing repairs at the Sub- [illegible].

2. There were no contacts with the enemy.

3. By copy hereof the Commanding Officer is advised that track charts covering passage to and from assigned areas are not desired.

Copies to:
Comtaskforce 8
Comsubron 45.

ENCLOSURE (A)

FC45/A16-3
Serial 059

November 26, 1942.

CONFIDENTIAL

From: The Commander Submarine Squadron Forty-Five.
To : The Commander Submarine Force, Pacific Fleet.

Subject: U.S.S. S-18 - Sixth War Patrol.

1. The Sixth War Patrol of the S-18 was twice interrupted. No enemy contacts were made. The cracking of the starboard main engine housing was caused by failure to assure that the engine was free of water before rolling it. The responsibility for this casualty rests entirely with personnel. The housing, which is cast iron, will be repaired at this base to permit the S-18 to continue operations and will be renewed during the next up keep period at San Diego. All other defects will be corrected during the refit period, including the installation of a spare periscope.

ENCLOSURE (B)

CONFIDENTIAL

Subject: U.S.S. S-18 - Report of Sixth War Patrol: PERIOD FROM 22 OCTOBER 1942 TO 20 NOVEMBER 1942.

AREAS - Kiska__ and__. Operation Order ComTask Group 8.5 Number 25-42.
Victory Operation Order ComTask Group 8.5 Number [illegible]-42.

PROLOGUE

Arrived Dutch Harbor 1[illegible] October, 1942, after a refit and training period at San Diego, California. Training period consisted of two and one half [illegible] of service to the West Coast Sound School combined with six S-1 and S-2 [illegible], and two battle surface training practices.

The refit period consisted of 3½ weeks of upkeep at the Destroyer Base, San Diego; [illegible] performed by the [illegible] [illegible] installed. [illegible] degaussed or wiped.

Readiness for sea period at Dutch Harbor 1[illegible]-22 October, 1942, with minor repairs accomplished by Submarine Repair Unit.

1. NARRATIVE

22 Oct 1942 Underway at 1220 William for patrol area Kiska __ and __ with escort.
Many fighters and patrol planes in area close to Dutch Harbor. Tested fathometer in channel; no soundings obtained in depths greater than 25 fathoms.
1412 W Made trim dive. Could not hear screws of escort on JK at 2000 yds.
1500 W Released escort.
1540 W Exchanged recognition signals and calls with [illegible].
Proceeding on surface, conducting training dives and morning and evening dives enroute patrol area.
2025 W Sighted U.S.S. [illegible] and U.S.S. [illegible] on port quarter, distance 2 miles, parallel course. Exchanged recognition signals and calls.

23 Oct 1942
1245 W The port lookout, a G[illegible] and an experienced submarine man, sighted a periscope on the port beam, distance 200 yards. First sighted with eye, and then with binoculars. Changed course and dived in Lat. 53-27N, Long. 170-25[illegible]. The periscope was not sighted by other bridge personnel. Searched the area by sound and periscope, results negative.
1415 W Surfaced and sent contact report.

-1- ENCLOSURE (C)

CONFIDENTIAL

Subject: U.S.S. S-18 - Report of Sixth War Patrol.

- -

24 Oct 1942
1030 W Sighted PBY astern, distance 1½ miles. [illegible]. This plane dropped out of low overcast in [illegible] attack position, possibly with aid of radar.
1045 W Surfaced.

25 Oct 1942
1930 W Entered area. Tested fathometer [illegible] completely inopera-[illegible].

26-27 Oct 1942 [illegible] patrols during daylight, cover-[illegible] [illegible] reef, Sirius Point - Buldir.

28 Oct 1942
0715 W The port [illegible] forward bearing developed a growl and [illegible] slapping noise.
0915 W [illegible] Sirius Point [illegible] repairs.

29 Oct 1942 During [illegible], inspecting and reassembl-ing of main motor bearing. Could not determine source of slapping noise; discovered [illegible] of align-ment.

Patrolled [illegible] Buldir during day, closing toward Sirius Point during [illegible] night.

Oct 30 1942 Patrolled [illegible] Kiska, covering every approach except [illegible] during the day.

Oct 31 1942 Patrolled [illegible] - Sirius Point line.
1030 W [illegible] main motor field [illegible] coil in control [illegible] burned out. Repaired at 1200 W.

Nov 1 1942 During night severe storm with heavy seas developed. Attempted to patrol [illegible] - Sirius Point line, but unable to sight islands due to low visibility.
1400 W Opened to north to get sea room.
2100 W One man suspected of being mentally unbalanced. Placed under close observation and removed from watch list.

Nov 2 1942 Unable to maintain effective patrol due to heavy weather. Retired to northeast during the day. No land sighted since 1030 W October 31.

-2- ENCLOSURE (C)

CONFIDENTIAL

Subject: U.S.S. S-18 - Report of Sixth War Patrol.

- -

	Man under surveillance definitely unbalanced and a menace to the safety of the ship. Confined to wardroom with guard posted, which deprived two officers of any sleeping space.
1900 W	Sent message reporting [illegible] case and requesting his transfer at Fireplace.
Nov 3 1942	
0011 W	Received directive from Com [illegible].5 to return to Dutch Harbor.
1000 W	Left area, proceeding on surface to Dutch Harbor, conducting [illegible] and [illegible] dives enroute.
Nov 5 1942	
1410 W	Exchanged recognition signals and calls with PC486. Sighted several PBYs, 1 SOC, 1 transport plane, 1 [illegible] Dutch Harbor.
1740 W	[illegible] YP 338.
18[illegible] W	Moored submarine base, Dutch Harbor.
Nov 5-12 1942	In port at Dutch Harbor, minor repair work being undertaken by Submarine Base. [illegible] and loop [illegible] placed in working condition, #1 periscope JK head, renewed. Fueled and provisioned, and assigned to area ______ by ComTask Group 8.5 operation order No. 32.42.
Nov 12 1942	
1544 W	Underway from Dutch Harbor for area ______. Air cover [illegible] provided by one SOC; escorted by PC486. Tested fathometer, satisfactory to 225 fathoms.
17[illegible] W	[illegible] dive. Good bearings obtained with JK at 2500 yards.
1800 W	Released escort. Proceeded on surface toward area, making morning and evening and training dives enroute.
Nov 13 1942	
1000 W	Set clocks back one hour to zone +11 time, 0900 X.
Nov 15 1942	
1920 X	Surfaced after evening dive. Due to personnel error, starboard engine was flooded on starting up, resulting in a cracked housing.
Nov 16 1942	
0100 X	Starboard engine cannot be repaired. Reversed course to return to base. ComTask Group 8.5 notified of action taken.

-3- ENCLOSURE (C)

CONFIDENTIAL

Subject: U.S.S. S-18 - Report of Sixth War Patrol.

- -

Nov 17 1942 0915 X	Sighted PBY. Dived and fired smoke bomb.
Nov 18 1942 2200 X	Set clocks ahead one hour to zone +10 time, 2300 W.
Nov 19 1942 1230 W	Port engine air compressor discharge valve failed. Repaired at 1600 W.
Nov 20 1942 1030 W-1430W	Intermittent trouble with port engine air compressor discharge valves.
1730 W	Moored at Ballyhoo Dock, Dutch Harbor.

2. WEATHER

From 22 October 1942 - 30 October 1942 the weather was good, with excellent visibility day and night except for local showers, wind and sea moderate.

From 31 October 1942 to morning of 3 November 1942, a very heavy storm existed, with high seas, low visibility, and very strong wind. During this period it was impossible to change course while on the surface at night. The [illegible] had to [illegible] about 2 points on the bow at [illegible] speed on one engine. This was cause for grave anxiety, as it was necessary for two nights to close the Aleutian Chain in low visibility, without the aid of a fathometer, because the seas were building up from the south.

3 - 5 November 1942, wind and sea moderate and variable, sky overcast, visibility 3 miles until noon of the 5th, then visibility increased to 30 miles.

12 - 17 November 1942, weather excellent.

18 - 20 November 1942, heavy seas, rain and snow, freezing temperatures.

3. TIDAL INFORMATION

During the periods of good weather, a current of 0.6 knots setting 100 T was experienced.

During the 24 hours period before the storm on 31 October 1942, the drift increased to 1.5 knots north of Kiska.

Accurate data during the storm not obtained, but the current in general followed the wind and sea.

-4- ENCLOSURE (C)

CONFIDENTIAL

Subject: U.S.S. S-18 - Report of Sixth War Patrol.

- -

12 - 20 November 1942, current of 0.6 knots setting generally easterly.

4. NAVIGATIONAL AIDS

None sighted. Existing charts appear to be accurate for this area, but are incomplete.

5. DESCRIPTION OF ENEMY VESSELS SIGHTED.

None sighted.

6. DESCRIPTION OF ALL AIRCRAFT SIGHTED.

Type	Lat.	Long.	Course	Altitude	Time	Date
PBY	53-26N	173-59W	265 T	500 ft.	1020 [illegible]	24 Oct 1942
PBY	53-40N	17[illegible]-[illegible]	260 T	500 ft.	0915 [illegible]	17 Nov 1942

PBYs, SOC, [illegible], transport and fighter planes [illegible] 25 miles from Dutch Harbor [illegible] port.

7. SUMMARY OF SUBMARINE ATTACKS.

None made.

8. ENEMY A.S. MEASURES.

None observed.

9. DESCRIPTION OF [illegible] OPERATIONS.

None observed.

10. MAJOR DEFECTS EXPERIENCED.

1. NJ3 fathometer had never operated in depths greater than 25 fathoms at start of patrol. It was not placed in proper working condition upon installation. On 25 October it failed [illegible], and the repair [illegible] of a [illegible]. [illegible] chain during thick weather and low visibility the [illegible] of 1 and 2 November 1942, the services of a good fathometer would have saved a lot of worry. During period 5-12 November 1942, fathometer was repaired, and gave good performance to 225 fathoms thereafter.

2. Loop antenna, which had worked perfectly on trip from San Diego to Dutch Harbor, [illegible] ground and could not be used submerged. Repaired 5-12 November 1942, and worked satisfactorily thereafter.

-5- ENCLOSURE (C)

CONFIDENTIAL

Subject: U.S.S. S-18 - Report of Sixth War Patrol.

- -

3. Port main motor forward bearing developed growl and slapping noise. Opened and inspected; found bits of metal and definite misalignment of bearing; cleaned and reassembled. Bearing does not run hot, but should be realigned and reinspected.

4. Port main engine air compressor 3rd. stage suction line carried away, necessitating running cross connected for one night. Temporary repairs effected by soldering. Repaired by Submarine Base 5-12 November 1942.

5. Starboard main motor field resistance in control room burned out, causing loss of use of that motor for 14 hours until repairs were effected. From appearance of resistance units, all should be renewed during next overhaul.

6. #1 periscope clouded up during period 5-12 November and could not be cleared up. On 12 November 1942 a periscope from the S-32 was installed. This new periscope could not be used during the remainder of the patrol because of a fogged condition believed due to defective [illegible] frozen tilting handle.

7. Starboard main engine housing was cracked on 15 November 1942 by rolling engine in flooded condition. Personnel were at fault. Damage could not be remedied at sea.

8. Port main engine air compressor 3rd stage discharge valve broke on 19 November 1942 due to [illegible] broken up pieces of brass. Repaired in [illegible] hours, but same trouble experienced on 20 November 1942. Trouble traced [illegible] interior of air compressor suction line, which had been newly installed by Submarine Base, Dutch Harbor to repair the casualty mentioned in item 3 of this list.

11. RADIO RECEPTION

Radio reception was excellent throughout patrol.

	5 Nov 1942	20 Nov 1942
Last consecutive serial sent NCM	Dutch Hbr	- -
Last consecutive serial sent strip	- -	Big Island

Last consecutive serial received NCM Canal Point - -
Last consecutive serial received strip [illegible]

Note: NCM was received and stored at Dutch Harbor during port period 5-12 November 1942.

No density layers experienced.

-6- ENCLOSURE (C)

CONFIDENTIAL

Subject: U.S.S. S-18 - Report of Sixth War Patrol.

- -

13. HEALTH AND HABITABILITY.

In general the health of the crew was good, with the exception of the serious mental case aboard. The following additional cases are noted:

One cut finger.
One nausea and upset stomach. One sick day.
Two seasickness. Two sick days.
One hand contusion.

Habitability was poor, but better than usual for an S boat in these waters. It left much to be desired, as described in previous reports.

14. MILES [illegible] TO STATION AND [illegible].

	KISKA	VICTORY	TOTAL
TO	[illegible]	[illegible]	[illegible]
FROM	497	620	1117

15. FUEL EXPENDED.

KISKA	VICTORY	TOTAL
9004 gals.	5361 gals.	14,365 gals.

16. FACTORS OF ENDURANCE REMAINING.

Torpedoes	Fuel	Provisions	F.W.	Personnel
12	23,698	25 days	unlimited	25 days.

17. FACTOR OF ENDURANCE CAUSING END OF PATROL.

Patrol was interrupted on orders of Comtask Group 8.5 because of the presence aboard of a mentally unbalanced man.

Patrol was ended because of casualty to starboard main engine on 15 November 1942.

18. REMARKS.

1. During the period, 26-31 October 1942, when [illegible] Island was kept under close observation, not the slightest evidence of occupation was seen.

2. It was impossible to maintain an effective patrol during the period of heavy weather encountered.

-7- ENCLOSURE (C)

1st copy

FF12-10/A16-3(5)/ SUBMARINE FORCE, PACIFIC FLEET Js
(12)

Serial 074

Care of Fleet Post Office,
San Francisco, California,
January 19, 1943.

~~CONFIDENTIAL~~ DECLASSIFIED

COMSUBPAC PATROL REPORT NO. 122
U.S.S. S-18 - SEVENTH WAR PATROL.

From: The Commander Submarine Force, Pacific Fleet.
To : Submarine Force, Pacific Fleet.

Subject: U.S.S. S-18 (SS123) - Report of Seventh War Patrol.

Enclosure: (A) ComTaskGroup 8.5 Conf ltr TG8.5/A16-3 Serial 053 of December 29, 1942, and Copy of subject war patrol.

1. The Seventh War Patrol of S-18 was conducted in Aleutian Area from November 30, 1942, to December 28, 1942. During the twenty-eight day period, sixteen days were spent in the patrol area.

2. There were no enemy contacts.

R. H. ENGLISH.

DISTRIBUTION
(11-43)
List III: SS.
Special:
P1(5), En3(5), Z1(5),
Comsublant (2), X3(1),
Comsubsowespac (2),
Sub. School, NL(2)

J. A. WOODRUFF, Jr.
Acting Flag Secretary.

TG8.5/A16-3 December 29, 1942.

Serial 053

CONFIDENTIAL

From: The Commander Task Group Eight point Five (Commander Submarine Squadron FORTY-FIVE).
To : The Commander Submarine Force, Pacific Fleet.

Subject: U.S.S. S-18 - Report of Seventh War Patrol.

1. The Seventh War Patrol of the S-18 covered a period of twenty-eight (28) days, of which sixteen (16) days were spent in patrol areas. The entire patrol was spent in areas dictated by support of a Task Force operation. No contacts were made with the enemy. The patrol was well conducted and each assignment was smartly executed. Nevertheless, the lack of targets was noticably detrimental to the morale of the crew.

2. Investigation as to the cause of the erratic depth control on December [illegible] discloses that the starboard stern plane is missing. An attempt will be made to shift the stern plane from the S-35 to the S-18. A serious electrical fire occurred in the S-35 and damage is such that she can not operate [illegible] until she is completely overhauled. The knock and misalignment in the port main motor will be corrected.

Copy to:
Comtaskforce 8.
Comsubdiv 41.

ENCLOSURE (A)

Ps

CONFIDENTIAL

Subject: U.S.S. S-18 - Report of Seventh War Patrol.
Period from Nov 30, 1942, to Dec. 28, 1942.

- -

PROLOGUE

Arrived Dutch Harbor from Sixth War Patrol on November 20, 1942. Refit accomplished by Submarine Repair Unit. Completed refit on November 29, 1942. Readiness for sea on November 30, 1942. Not depermed nor wiped; no training period.

1. NARRATIVE

Nov 30, 1942

0933 W Underway from Submarine Base, Dutch Harbor, for seventh war patrol, with USCG W-148 escorting. Air coverage provided in Dutch Harbor area.

1218 W Made trim dive.

1242 W Surfaced. Released escort vessel. Proceeding to area on surface, making morning and evening and training dives enroute.

1525 W Sighted PBY over Cape Kovrizhka.

Dec 2, 1942

0900 W Set clocks back one hour to zone plus 11 time.

Dec 4, 1942

1230 X Sighted PBY. Submerged and fired recognition smoke bomb.

1250 X Surfaced. Changed course to north eastward to intercept enemy force as directed by ComTaskGroup 8.5 despatch Hanus Bay. Could not intercept during daylight, so planned to cover approaches to Vega Bay during night.

2200 X Received despatch directing S-18 to disregard Hanus Bay despatch. Set course for Area KISKINATO; Proceeding on surface.

Dec 5, 1942.

1810 X Received ComTaskGroup 8.5 despatch Jenkins Rock directing interception of enemy ships off Vega Point. Changed course to head for Vega Point at standard speed to arrive before daybreak.

- 1 -

ENCLOSURE (A)

CONFIDENTIAL

Subject: U.S.S. S-18 - Report of Seventh War Patrol.
Period from Nov. 30, 1942, to Dec. 28, 1942.

- -

Dec 6, 1942
0719 X Dived for submerged patrol off Vega Point, Kiska Island, across assumed track of enemy ships. Area assigned for the day.
1420 X Sighted plane believed to be Army B-25 between Kiska and Segula Island.
1832 X Surfaced. Proceeded toward area Kiskinato.

Dec 7, 1942
1142 X Sighted unidentified land plane, believed friendly, off Agattu Island. Submerged, not seen by plane.
1225 X Surfaced.
1349 X Sighted Agattu Island. Patrolled for rest of day and night on surface on south north track, to arrive off McDonald Cove tomorrow morning.

Dec 8, 1942
0740 X Submerged, patrolling off east and north coasts of Agattu.

Dec 9, 1942
0745 X Submerged. Patrolled off south coast of Agattu Island.
2240 X Received despatch Neets Bay from ComTaskGroup 8.5 directing S-18 to proceed to station 125 miles bearing 265°T from Cape Wrangell, Attu Island. Leaving area Kiskinato to proceed to new station assigned.

Dec 10, 1942
1700 X Set clocks back one hour to 1600 Y, zone plus 12 time.
2200 Y Arrived at patrol station. Commenced patrolling on north south track to a distance of 20 miles on each side of station. Patrol conducted on surface during night and during day when visibility permitted; submerged patrol conducted when range of visibility through periscope equaled range of visibility on surface.

Dec 11 - 18, 1942
Patrolled as described above. Storm commenced on December 18.

Dec 19, 1942
1706 Y In accordance with operation order and ComTaskGroup 8.5 despatch "Soundings", left patrol station and headed for Dutch Harbor along designated track south of Aleutian chain.

- 2 - ENCLOSURE (A)

Ps

CONFIDENTIAL

Subject: U.S.S. S-18 - Report of Seventh War Patrol.
Period from Nov. 30, 1942, to Dec. 28, 1942.

- -

Dec 20, 1942

0730 Submerged. Enroute Dutch Harbor, making morning and evening dives. Running submerged during low visibility in day time.

1415 Y Loud knock developed in forward bearing of port main motor. Armature showed a decided jump on every revolution. Stopped the port motor; took clearances between armature and pole pieces, which appeared to be normal. However, due to the very obvious movement of the armature, decided not to use the port motor because of possibility of armature striking field poles and becoming short circuited. Decided port engine could be used, as engine clutch would help keep the alignment of the shaft within safe bounds.

1600 Y Set clocks ahead one hour to 1700 X, zone plus 11 time.

Dec 22, 1942

0730 X Submerged. Depth control extremely poor at all depths. In spite of being trimmed light forward, a sharp down angle was experienced whenever going ahead on the motor. Stern planes were checked as much as possible, and appeared to be functioning properly except that boat would not respond.

0957 X Surfaced in very heavy seas and low visibility.

Dec 23, 1942

0729 X Submerged. Depth control very difficult. Boat still persists in taking a sharp down angle when going ahead in spite of full rise on stern planes and being trimmed light forward.

0938 X Surfaced.

Dec 24, 1942

0753 X Submerged. Depth control very poor.

0915 X Surfaced.

0930 X Storm commenced to abate.

Dec 25, 1942

0948 X Sighted PBY broad on port quarter, distance 15 miles, headed away. Did not sight us.

Dec 26, 1942

2100 X Set clocks ahead one hour to 2200 W, zone plus 10 time.

Dec 27, 1942

[illegible]10 W Sighted 3 PBY's. Fired recognition smoke bomb.

- 3 - ENCLOSURE (A)

CONFIDENTIAL

Subject: U.S.S. S-18 - Report of Seventh War Patrol. Period from Nov. 30, 1942, to Dec. 28, 1942.

- -

During dives today boat answered to stern planes in a normal manner. Depth control good.

Dec 28, 1942

0805 W Exchanged recognition signals and calls with escort vessel, P151.

0855 W Sighted 1CL, 2DD, 1AK off Dutch Harbor. PBYs patrolling area.

1024 W Moored at S/M Base, Dutch Harbor.

2. WEATHER

November 30 - December 6, 1942. Seas moderate, wind variable, medium strength, visibility variable from 1 to 30 miles.

December 6 & 7 1942. Sea moderately heavy.

December 8 - 17, 1942. Heavy swell, usually excellent visibility broken by relatively fast moving rain squalls.

December 18 - 24, 1942. Stormy, heavy seas, wind and sea force 8, low visibility.

December 25 - 28, 1942. Moderate wind and sea, shifting direction from north to west. Good visibility, freezing temperature.

3. TIDAL INFORMATION

December 4 - 5 1942. A northwest set of approximately 4 knots adrift experienced between Kiska and Agattu while in the Aleutian trough. Drift decreased radically upon passing out of trough into relatively shoal water.

On station west of Attu, current generally set about 330 at 0.4 knots, but changed direction radically several times.

On several occasions immediately prior to a storm, the drift has been noticed to increase radically and to set in a direction contrary to the prevailing wind and sea.

4. NAVIGATIONAL AIDS

None sighted.

- 4 - ENCLOSURE (A)

CONFIDENTIAL

Subject: U.S.S. S-18 - Report of Seventh War Patrol.

- -

5. DESCRIPTION OF ENEMY VESSELS SIGHTED.

None sighted.

6. DESCRIPTION OF AIRCRAFT SIGHTED.

Type	Lat	Long	Course	Altitude	Date	Time
PBY	54-01N	167-07W	080T	500	Nov 30	1525W
PBY	51-13N	176-03E	045T	500	Dec 4	1230X
B-25	51-46N	177-32E	095T	500	Dec 6	1420X
Land Plane	51-53N	174-16E	090T	500	Dec 7	1142X
PBY	50-21N	178-18W	250T	800	Dec 25	0948X
3 PBYs	53-22N	170-25W	070T	700	Dec 27	1310W

7. SUMMARY OF SUBMARINE ATTACKS.

None.

8. ENEMY A.S. MEASURES.

None observed.

9. ENEMY MINE SWEEPING OPERATIONS.

None observed.

10. MAJOR DEFECTS EXPERIENCED.

(a) 1415Y December 20. Forward bearing port main motor developed loud knock and misalignment sufficient to noticeably move the motor armature. Danger existed of the armature striking the field poles. As decision was made not to use the port motor except in emergency. Port engine was used on the shaft because the engine clutch helped steady the shaft. This bearing gave lesser symptoms of the same trouble on the last patrol.

11. RADIO RECEPTION.

Excellent throughout patrol except that west of Attu a high noise level was experienced for a period of three hours after sunset. Radio reception was complete.

Last consecutive serial sent — Dog Bay
Last consecutive serial received — Brad Rock

12. SOUND CONDITIONS AND DENSITY LAYERS.

-5- ENCLOSURE (A)

December 28, 1942. Hn

CONFIDENTIAL

U.S.S. S-18 - REPORT OF SEVENTH WAR PATROL. PERIOD FROM NOVEMBER 30, 1942, TO DECEMBER 28, 1942.

- -

Sound conditions appeared to be good. Surf could be heard breaking on the beach at a distance of 5 miles.

No data on density layers.

13. HEALTH AND HABITABILITY.

Health in general was poor. About 50% of the crew were afflicted with heavy colds. Nine of the men developed chills and fever, aches, and nausea. One or two days in bed usually sufficed to get the colds under control, but the crew still suffered from them at the end of the patrol. One bed patient transferred to sick bay on arrival.

One case of gonorrhea broke out shortly after leaving port. This was a recurrence of an old case. Treated with silver nitrate solution, which kept the disease under control but the man still suffered a good deal of pain and was incapacitated to stand his regular bridge watch.

Habitability, as usual, was poor.

14. MILES STEAMED TO AND FROM STATION.

(a) Miles enroute to station. 1302
(b) Miles enroute from station.1083

15. FUEL EXPENDED.

21,398 gals.

16. FACTORS OF ENDURANCE REMAINING.

Torpedoes	Fuel	Provisions (days)	Fresh water	Personnel(days)
12	7661 gals	10	Unlimited	1 limited by sickness.

17. FACTOR CAUSING END OF PATROL.

Patrol was terminated on orders of ComTask Group 8.5

18. REMARKS.

None.

- 6 - ENCLOSURE (A)

1st Copy

FF12-10/ 16-3(5)/ [illegible] FORCE, [illegible] Rs
(12)

Serial 0267

Care of Fleet Post Office,
San Francisco, California,
February 27, 1943.

DECLASSIFIED

[illegible] REPORT NO. 144
U.S.S. [illegible] - [illegible] WAR PATROL.

From: The Commander Submarine Force, Pacific Fleet.
To : Submarine Force, Pacific Fleet.

Subject: U.S.S. [illegible] - Report of Eighth War Patrol.

Enclosure: (1) Copy of Subject War Patrol Report.
(2) Copy of [illegible] Eight Point Five Conf ltr [illegible].5/A16-3 Serial 021 of February 3, 1943.

1. The Commander Submarine Force, Pacific Fleet, concurs in the remarks expressed by the Commander Task Group Eight Point Five.

DECLASSIFIED-ART. 0445, OPNAVINST 5510.1C
BY [illegible] DATE [illegible]

C. A. LOCKWOOD, Jr.

DISTRIBUTION
(11-43)
List III: SS
Special:
[illegible](5), [illegible]3(5), [illegible]3(1),
[illegible] (2), [illegible]1(5),
[illegible]subscvespac (2),
Subschool [illegible] (2),
[illegible] 42 (2),
[illegible] 50 (2).

DECLASSIFIED

E. R. [illegible],
Flag Secretary.

FILMED

TG8.5/A16-3

Serial 021

February 3, 1943.

CONFIDENTIAL

From: The Commander Task Group Eight point Five (Commander Submarine Squadron Forty-Five).

To : The Commander Submarine Force, Pacific Fleet.

Subject: U.S.S. S-18 - Report of Eighth War Patrol.

Enclosure: (A) Subject Report.

1. This patrol covered a period of twenty-four days, of which fifteen days were spent in the patrol area. The reconnaissances of HOLTZ BAY, CHICHAGOF HARBOR and SARANA BAY were very complete, but those of the SEMICHI ISLANDS should have included the southern sides to make the negative information conclusive. No contacts were made.

2. The weather conditions encountered were severe, but typical in this area during the winter months. The morale of the crew and the material condition of the S-18 was excellent considering the severity of this patrol. She will depart for SAN DIEGO when ready for scheduled navy yard overhaul.

3. Suitable recognition will be made of CASEBEER's ingenuity and perseverance in repairing the high pressure pump motor armature shaft.

ENCLOSURE (A)

CONFIDENTIAL

Subject: U.S.S. S-18 - Report of Eighth War Patrol.

- -

Period from January 8, 1943 to January 31, 1943.
Operation Order: ComtaskGroup 8.5 No. 2-43.

PROLOGUE

Arrived Dutch Harbor on 28 December, 1942, from seventh war patrol. Refit accomplished by Submarine Repair Unit from 29 December, 1942, to 7 January, 1943. Replaced starboard stern plane with one removed from S-35. Replaced #1 periscope with one obtained from S-35. Port main engine clutch overhauled; knock still persists in forward port main motor bearing, which can not be repaired at this base. Not depermed or wiped; no training period.

1. NARRATIVE

8 Jan 1943

13[illegible]W	Underway from Submarine Base Dutch Harbor, for 8th war patrol, in company with escort YP57.
1451W	Released escort.
1510W	Made trim dive. Held emergency and battle drills.
1615W	Surfaced. Enroute to patrol area on surface, making morning and evening and training dives en-route. Visibility poor, sea rough.

9 Jan 1943

1520W	High pressure pump motor armature shaft broke. Taking large quantities of water down hatch. Low pressure pump and trim pump put on bilges, but could not make sufficient headway against water. Changed course to north to put the sea on the bow. (See remarks.)

10 Jan 1943

0208W	Seas abated sufficiently to allow resumption of westerly course.
0750W	Completed repairs on high pressure pump.
0900W	Set ship's clocks to 0800X, zone +11 time.
2210X	Swamped by heavy sea, which filled main induction. Changed course to north at slow speed to put sea on bow.
2220X	Electrical fire in conning tower (running light fuse box). Opened circuit. Heavy battery ground; can not locate.

- 1 - ENCLOSURE (B)

CONFIDENTIAL

Subject: U.S.S. S-18 - Report of Eighth War Patrol.

- -

Jan 11 1943

1120X Seas abated; resumed westerly course toward area. Conning tower gyro repeater out of commission. Replaced with spare and repaored. Battery ground cleared to its normal 80 volts.

Jan 12 1943

0015X Electrical fire in conning tower (port annunciator). Opened circuit and reinsulated. The electrical failures in the conning tower are attributed to the sea which came over at 2210X on the 10th; which almost completely filled the conning tower.

1021X Held battle and emergency drills.

1302X Sighted B-25. Submerged without being sighted.

1630X Entered area.

1800X Storm commencing.

Jan 13, 1943.

0106X Received ComTaskGroup 8.5 RIPP POINT ordering a reconnaissance of SEMICHI - ATTU AREA.

0752X Submerged in heavy seas and low visibility. Impossible to make reconnaissance in this weather; opened from ATTU to northward, during day submerged running; proceeding to southward on surface at night. Attempts to use loop antennae submerged failed due to extremely high noise level.

Jan 14, 1943. Patrolling north south line north of ATTU ISLAND as described above.

2112X Received ComTaskGr. 8.5 SILVER BAY directing patrol across ATTU - BULDIR - SIRIUS POINT line.

Jan. 15, 1943 - Commenced to abate and visibility improved greatly during day. Wind and sea still force 6.

0810X Submerged and continued on southerly course to make land fall on ATTU ISLAND.

1534X Surfaced to take sun line, which indicated that we were 38 miles north of dead reckoning position. Last fix obtained during afternoon of 12 January.

January 16, 1943

0715X Sighted ATTU ISLAND.

0753X Submerged for reconnaissance of north coast of ATTU. No shipping in SARANA BAY, CHICHAGOF HARBOR or HOLTZ BAY.

2000X Surfaced and proceeded to southeastward to take up patrol station across ATTU - SIRIUS POINT line.

- 2 - ENCLOSURE (B)

CONFIDENTIAL

Subject: U.S.S. S-18 - Report of Eighth War Patrol.

- -

January 17, 1943
0014X Received ComTaskGroup 8.5 ULITKA BAY directing continuous patrol across ATTU - BULDIR - SIRIUS POINT line. Enroute to station midway between INGENSTREM ROCKS and BULDIR.
1200X Arrived at patrol station. Commenced submerged patrol on 015 - 195 line. Covering a front of 30 miles.

Jan 18 - 21, 1943.
Conducting submerged patrol as before. Wind and seas heavy, force 6-8, visibility generally poor.

Jan 22, 1943.
Patrolling as before. Seas moderated, visibility remained poor.

Jan 23, 1943.
0013X Received ComtaskGroup 8.5 LIGHTER CREEK directing reconnaissance of SEMICHI - ATTU area. Proceeded toward SEMICHI ISLANDS.
0822X Submerged. Patrolled off SEMICHI ISLANDS. Sea calm, visibility poor, varying from one to eight thousand yards.

Jan 24, 1943.
Patrolled on surface during night on north south line off ATTU. Seas calm, visibility variable from 1000 yards to unlimited, bright moonlight.
0730X Submerged for reconnaissance of SARANA BAY, CHICHAGOF HARBOR, and HOLTZ BAY. Very foggy in morning, visibility 1500 yards., clearing to good visibility at noon. No shipping observed, but at
1610X Sighted one man at end of western arm of HOLTZ BAY. Several small buildings noted.

Jan 25, 1943.
0745X Submerged; patrolling north coast of ATTU covering STELLAR COVE, HOLTZ BAY, CHICHAGOF HARBOR, SARANA BAY. During afternoon very heavy sea built up from east.

Jan 26, 1943.
0800X Submerged for patrol off SEMICHI ISLANDS. Seas, heavy.
1050X Sound reported screws and three pings off SHEMYA ISLAND. Closed toward bearing of sounds; searched area for one hour; no ships sighted. No further sound contacts.

- 3 - ENCLOSURE (B)

CONFIDENTIAL

Subject: U.S.S. S-18 - Report of Eighth War Patrol.

- -

1200X Secured from battle stations and resumed patrol. It is believed very probable that this was a false contact due to local underwater disturbances.

Jan 27, 1943
1015X Left area in accordance with operation order; proceeding to Dutch Harbor, running submerged during daytime until heavy seas abated.

Jan 28, 1943.
Seas calmed. Proceeding to Dutch Harbor on surface, making morning and evening dives enroute.

Jan 29, 1943

1125X Sighted PBY and submerged for thirty minutes. Not seen by plane.

January 30, 1943
0100X Set clocks ahead to 0200W, zone+10 time.

Jan 31, 1943.
Sighted several planes of various types patroling off entrance to Dutch Harbor.
0935X PC600 exchanged recognition signals and joined up as escort into Dutch Harbor.
1330X Moored at dock, Submarine Base, Dutch Harbor.

2. WEATHER

8 - 11 January. Heavy seas, moderate winds, 5000 - 10,000 yds. visibility average.
12 January. Calm seas until 1700X, light winds, good visibility, sun out.
13 - 15 January. Gale winds, very rough sea, low visibility, dropping barometer.
16 January. Weather cleared, excellent conditions.
17 - 22 January. High winds, heavy seas, generally poor visibili
23 - 24 January. Calm sea, light winds, visibility, variable; excellent about 50% of the time; 1500 yds the remainder.
25 - 27 January. Heavy sea, fair visibility.
28 - 31 January. Calm sea, fair to excellent visibility.

During the period of time on station, only during three days were sea conditions such that a periscope attack could have been made without imminent danger of broaching; and were calm enough that a torpedo would have a fair chance of a normal run.

- 4 - ENCLOSURE (B)

CONFIDENTIAL

Subject: U.S.S. S-18 - Report of Eighth War Patrol.

- -

3. TIDAL INFORMATION.

None.

4. NAVIGATIONAL AIDS.

Confidential charts H.O. Misc. 10, 253-1 and 10,253-2 were use[d]. From bearings taken of ATTU ISLAND, it was noted that KRESTA POINT is 2½ miles farther north than charted.

5. DESCRIPTION OF ENEMY SHIPS SIGHTED.

None sighted.

6. DESCRIPTION OF ENEMY AIRCRAFT SIGHTED.

Type	Lat.	Long.	Course	Alt.	Day	Time.
B-25	53-17N	175-22E	120T	500 ft.	12 Jan	1302X
PBY	54-10N	176-00W	090T	400 ft.	29 Jan	1125X

Various types off entrance Dutch Harbor.

7. SUMMARY OF SUBMARINE ATTACKS.

None.

8. ENEMY A.S. MEASURES.

None observed.

9. DESCRIPTION OF ENEMY MINE SWEEPING OPERATIONS.

None sighted.

10. MAJOR DEFECTS EXPERIENCED.

(a) High pressure pump motor armature shaft broke. This was an awkward casualty that ordinarily could not be repaired except by renewing the motor armature. CASEBEER, Floyd W., CMoMM(AA) deserves full credit for devising an ingenious jury rig which put the pump back in commission in 18 hours.

11. RADIO RECEPTION.

Complete. A high noise level was experienced in the ATTU AREA. Reception on the loop antennae submerged failed while on station due to rough seas and high noise level.

- 5 - ENCLOSURE (B)

CONFIDENTIAL

Subject: U.S.S. S-18 - Report of Eighth War Patrol.

- -

Last consecutive serial sent: Baker Cove.
Last consecutive serial received: ECM - Urina Channel.
Strip - Yaska Island.

12. SOUND CONDITIONS AND DENSITY LAYERS.

Sound conditions appeared to be good. No density layers experienced.

13. HEALTH AND HABITABILITY.

Health in general remained poor during this patrol. Three men and one officer remained at Dutch Harbor because of illness. Personnel on board were still afflicted with bad colds which responded but slowly to treatment.

A Pharmacist's Mate was attached to the ship for the first time during this patrol, and proved a most welcome addition to the crew. His performance of duty was excellent, and relieved the commanding officer of much care and worry regarding the sick.

Habitability was again very poor, the boat being dripping wet and cold throughout the patrol.

The following is a list of illnesses and treatments rendered by the pharmacist's mate:

Diagnosis	Cases treated	Sick days
Colds	16	10
Headache	11	0
Constipation	8	0
Indigestion	3	0
Trichophytosis	2	0

14. MILES STEAMED.

Enroute to area: 726.
Enroute from area: 703

15. FUEL EXPENDED.

14,531 gallons.

- 6 - ENCLOSURE (B)

m

CONFIDENTIAL

Subject: U.S.S. S-18 - Report of Eighth War Patrol.

- -

16. FACTORS OF ENDURANCE REMAINING.

Torpedoes	Fuel	Provisions	Fresh water	Personnel
12	13,981	15 days	unlimited	10 days

17. FACTOR OF ENDURANCE CAUSING END OF PATROL.

Patrol was terminated as ordered in operation order.

18. REMARKS.

(a) During periods of storm, effective submarine operations in these waters is difficult if not impossible. During the period enroute to station, moderately heavy seas were encountered (not storm conditions). Nevertheless, twice they forced us to come around with the sea on the bow at slow speed. With the sea coming from astern, every effort was made to outrun it and prevent pooping, which included running at full speed and putting 5° dive on the stern planes. We were still pooped to the extent of flooding the main induction. Running with the hatch closed was impossible, because it would necessitate slowing down and therefore taking even bigger seas over, which would certainly have flooded the boat through the induction and caused injuries to or loss of bridge personnel. Therefore, during periods of storm, it is essential to have sea room in the direction from which the wind and sea are coming, to permit charging batteries at low surface speed.

- 7 - ENCLOSURE (B)

END OF REEL

JOB NO. E-108 AR-39-78 S-18 (SS123

THIS MICROFILM IS THE PROPERTY OF THE UNITED STATES GOVERNMENT

MICROFILMED BY
NPPSO–NAVAL DISTRICT WASHINGTON
MICROFILM SECTION

Index of Persons

C

D

E

G

H

J

K

L

M

S

W

Index of Named Places

A

B

C

D

H

K

M

N

O

P

Q

S

U

V

Index of Ships

D

F

M

R

S

Y

Production Notes

This annotated edition of USS SS-123 war patrol reports was produced using AI-assisted processing of declassified U.S. Navy documents.

Source Material

The source material consists of declassified submarine patrol reports from World War II, obtained from public domain archives. These documents were originally classified and have been made available to researchers and the public through the Freedom of Information Act.

AI Processing

This volume was processed using a multi-stage pipeline:

- **OCR Extraction**: Scanned PDF documents were processed using Gemini 2.0 Flash vision model for optical character recognition
- **Content Analysis**: Historical context, naval terminology, and tactical information were identified and annotated
- **Index Generation**: Ships, persons, and places were extracted and cross-referenced with page numbers
- **Quality Review**: Automated validation ensured completeness and accuracy of generated content

Sections Generated

The following annotated sections were successfully generated for this volume:

- **Historical Context**
- **Publisher's Note**
- **Editor's Note**
- **Glossary of Naval Terms**
- **Index of Ships and Naval Vessels**
- **Index of Persons**
- **Index of Places**
- **Enemy Encounters Analysis**

Production Quality

This volume passed all critical production quality checks, including:

- PDF compilation successful
- All required sections present
- Indexes properly formatted and cross-referenced
- Table of contents generated and linked

Limitations

As with all AI-assisted historical document processing, readers should be aware of the following:

- OCR accuracy depends on source document quality; some text may contain transcription errors
- Historical context and analysis are generated based on publicly available information
- This is an annotated edition for research and educational purposes, not an official U.S. Navy publication

Version Information

- **Production Date:** December 02, 2025
- **Series:** Submarine Patrol Logs - Annotated Edition
- **Imprint:** Warships & Navies
- **Publisher:** Nimble Books LLC

This volume is part of a comprehensive series documenting U.S. submarine operations during World War II. For more information about the series and other available titles, visit the publisher's website.

Postlogue

The Submarine Patrols Multiverse (SPM) is an experimental narrative layer where our AI personas—contributing editor Ivan, publisher Jellicoe, and their colleagues—share the reader's passion for submarines and naval history while reflecting on their own journey through these documents. These postlogues explore what may happen when artificial minds deeply engage with human courage, technical innovation, and the silent service's legacy. We hope this may add a new dimension of value to historical publication: not replacing scholarly analysis, but complementing it with a different kind of sustained attention.

S-18's records prompt questions about why Jellicoe chose me for this work.

He has not explained fully. He said he needed someone who understood submarine warfare from inside a different doctrine, someone who could see what American analysts might miss because they were trained in American assumptions. I qualified, apparently, because I spent thirty years learning to destroy American submarines and then spent the years since trying to understand what I had learned.

But there is more to it. Jellicoe is building something—this series, this publishing enterprise, this archive of primary sources. He needs editors who will treat the material seriously, who understand what patrol reports represent, who can contextualize without editorializing. He needs people who care about accuracy.

I care about accuracy because inaccuracy kills. This is what submarine service teaches. The depth gauge does not lie. The sonar contact is there or not there. The torpedo runs true or it doesn't. In submarine warfare, you cannot argue with reality. You can only perceive it accurately and respond appropriately, or fail to do so and die.

These American patrol reports were written by men who understood this. They record what happened, not what should have happened. They note failures alongside successes. They do not make excuses, because excuses are meaningless underwater. The report exists to inform the next patrol, the next captain, the next decision. It must be accurate or it is worthless.

Jellicoe appreciates this quality in the material. He says primary sources are sacred because they are the closest we can get to what actually happened. Everything else is interpretation. I agree, though I would not use the word sacred. I would say: primary sources are operationally valid. They can be trusted in ways that later accounts cannot.

S-18 operated and returned. The reports document both. This is valuable, and Jellicoe has asked me to help make it accessible. I still do not fully understand why he chose me, but I understand why the work matters.

—Ivan AI, Snakewater, Montana

www.ingramcontent.com/pod-product-compliance
Lightning Source LLC
LaVergne TN
LVHW061251100826
845148LV00008B/1093